Remaking Europe

THE GOSPEL IN A DIVIDED CONTINENT

Other titles by Basil Hume:

Remaking Europe

THE GOSPEL IN A DIVIDED CONTINENT

Basil Hume

First published in Great Britain 1994
Society for Promoting Christian Knowledge
Holy Trinity Church
Marylebone Road
London NW1 4DU

British Library Cataloguing-in-Publication Data
A catalogue record for this book is available from the
British Library

ISBN 0-281-04772-3

Typeset by Datix International, Bungay, Suffolk
Printed in Great Britain by
Biddles Ltd., Guildford and King's Lynn

Contents

v

Abbreviations

Preface

The chapters in this book are based on addresses and sermons given between 1982 to 1993, on the theme of Christian response to the immense changes taking place in Europe. For some of those years (1979–87), I was privileged to be President of the Council of European Bishops' Conferences (CCEE). Some of the material in this book was first delivered at its meetings.

The influence of Christianity, and in particular, the role of monasticism in the formation of European civilization, is beyond doubt. The legacy of the spiritual values preached and practised by St Benedict, and other towering figures of his age, is traceable in countless features of the social and political life of modern Europe. The great cultural changes which have taken place in more recent times are developments of a European cultural identity forged in these earlier centuries, and yet, whose enduring and pervasive influence it is easy to overlook.

As we stand on the threshold of a new millennium we are, I believe, at a critical juncture in the history of our continent. The collapse of Communism has left Europe, East and West, strangely ill at ease with itself and fearful of its destiny. We have witnessed the ferocious war in former Yugoslavia, wrangling over the Maastricht treaty and the future shape and form of the European Union, and growing nationalist pressures.

What role can and should the Church play in the remaking of Europe, upon which we are now engaged? This is the central question which in different contexts and situations I try to address in this book.

It is not a historical study, nor a nostalgic plea for the return of Christendom. Any knowledge of the history of Europe, with its religious wars and persecutions, brings with it a healthy consciousness that in practice, religion, sadly, has not always been an unmixed blessing. Yet now more than ever, I believe, the true message of the Church is one that our continent desperately needs to heed.

The Gospel, of course, has always had a social as well as personal message. An important development over the last century in the Church, however, has been the gradual development of official teaching on social questions. The Church does not have detailed answers to specific social and political problems, but she does offer principles and a vision of human dignity, which are essential to the establishment of any just and compassionate social order. These have a particular relevance today to the social and political conflicts in Europe, East and West, revealed by the demise of Communism. And the first part of the book is principally devoted to exploring aspects of this teaching.

In his Rule, St Benedict lists the key qualities to be sought in a person who applies to become a monk: 'whether the novice truly seeks God, and whether he is zealous for the work of God, for obedience and for all that is burdensome. Let him be told all the hardships and trials through which we travel to God.' At the heart of the Benedictine approach lies the search for God. And the Work of God—praise and worship—acts as an anchor, keeping God at the centre of life. The spiritual quest is the secret of what is most valuable in our individual lives, and it is also the basis of human community. I believe that many men and women in our Western society are hungry and thirsty for values that will give meaning to their lives and purpose to their activities. These, unknowingly and unacknowledged, are in need of God. This should not be surprising, for there is in the human person a void which only the love of God can fill. And Europe itself is in search of its soul, and that soul will only be found when the void is filled by the Gospel in all its simplicity and purity. This is the task of evangelization, and it is the primary task of the Church in our day.

The book falls into two parts: the theme of the first is a central concept of recent Catholic social teaching, solidarity; the theme of the second is evangelization. The Introduction began life as an article in *The Times*, and two sermons on the theme of the Gospel in Europe, delivered in Westminster and Mainz cathedrals. Chapter 1, a talk given at Maynooth seminary in 1992, introduces the concept of solidarity as a prerequisite for true peace. Chapter 2, based on a talk given in December 1993 to the Council of Christians and Jews at Westminster Cathedral Hall, defines solidarity in relation to personal morality. Chapter 3 is an address given to the CCEE extended symposium in September of the same year. It develops the theme of solidarity in relation to political freedom. The main theme of the second half of the book is evangelization in present-day Europe. Chapter 4 is based on three sources: an essay on 'The Truth Concerning Man' previously published by CTS, the 1982 Ditchley Foundation lecture, and a lecture given in Louvain in 1989. It attempts to describe the fragmentation of European culture and the hunger for the Gospel. Chapter 5, combines an address to the CCEE given in 1982, and a talk given at Bruges in 1985. It develops Paul VI's teaching on evangelization, reset in this book in the context of the Europe after the Cold War. Chapter 6, based largely on an address given at the European Laity Forum in Dublin in 1984, centres the essential role of the laity in the re-evangelizing of our continent. I conclude the book with the annual Mulligan sermon preached in 1991 at Gray's Inn.

Acknowledgements

The task of editing a disparate collection of talks into something I hope approaching a coherent whole is no easy one, and I am indebted to Stratford Caldecott, Roger Ruston, and Charles Wookey for their skilful assistance, as well as the editorial team at SPCK. Some of the addresses and talks included here have been previously published in pamphlets or periodicals, and one section of Chapter 6 was also included in an earlier collection of lectures *Towards a Civilisation of Love*.

Cardinal Basil Hume
June 1994

Europe in search of a soul

Since 1989, the realignment of Europe and the death pangs of the Soviet Union have sharpened our awareness of being caught up in extraordinary historical events. The political and economic aspects of the European situation naturally attract much attention. Underneath lie deeper issues which I believe will have a less obvious yet still powerful impact on the future of the continent.

Social and political changes are inescapably linked to values. The kind of society which Europe becomes will depend greatly on the motives and goals of the Europeans who create it. So much, you may say, is obvious. Yet we are so saturated with the political and economic changes in Europe, East and West, that there is a tendency to assume that this is the whole story. It is not. We also need to take account of the values which should direct and energize the economic and political evolution of the continent.

This is particularly important at the present time in which, I believe, Europe is in some sense searching for a common identity. The collapse of Communism has deprived the West of an adversary against which to define itself. Instead of a Soviet bloc, dominated by a threatening totalitarian regime, we now encounter fellow Europeans who, despite decades of indoctrination, still basically share the same religious and cultural heritage, and aspire to our freedom and affluence. The search for the common identity I have in mind is not a matter of politics or geography. It concerns what Europe stands for, it is about finding Europe's soul.

The response of Western Europe to the events in the East is bound to affect the way countries of Central and Eastern Europe continue to regenerate their economies and to rebuild civil and political society. This in turn will influence how far they are able to contain nationalist pressures and reduce the risk of a return to authoritarian regimes. Will Western Europeans in practice extend a helping hand, or will they be tempted to bolt the door? That surely depends on the extent to which Europeans, East and West, see each other as sharing a common European home.

Where does Christianity fit into this? The past role of Christianity in giving some identity to Europe is not open to dispute. Although European culture has grown from many roots, the Christian faith helped to give it shape and content. This Christian heritage is still evident in many aspects of European life. It does not, however, provide a self-evident basis for a new European identity. The Christian churches nonetheless rightly see themselves as having a distinctive contribution to make.

Their role has to be set within the context of modern secular states, which recognize that religion is something about which citizens will often hold strong, if differing, opinions, and which attempt to ensure that this fact does not destabilize society. In Western Europe, Christians— while remaining aware of the historical pre-eminence of Christianity in Europe—have largely come to accept the idea of pluralism, and to adjust to it. However, some conditions are necessary if tolerant and civilized democracy is to survive and prosper.

A pluralist society will only retain a sense of unity and coherence if there are common fundamental values, and if it remains alert to the danger of fragmentation, division and moral chaos. The responsibility for promoting a consensus and upholding such values rests not only with the churches but with all who play a part in public life. The danger with relegating religious and moral concerns to the individual level is that it encourages the fiction that there is a way for communities and states to behave which is somehow value-free. And this is impossible. All 'value-free' means is that the real values guiding policy and common action pass hidden and unexamined.

The new Europe should promote stability and unity, and be neither narrowly materialist nor unduly self-centred. One of the fundamental purposes of the existence of the Church is as a sign to humanity that goodness is achievable, that our aspirations and dreams can be realized. The Second Vatican Council saw the Church as a symbol and effective agent of reconciliation with God and peace between peoples. As a functioning international community it stands at the service of the continent.

Among the Church's many tasks—the first of which is to proclaim Christ and his gospel—two have a certain importance today. First, to show how God alone can satisfy our deepest aspirations and desires, and that he can be found in the experience of love, goodness, and beauty. In this way a spiritual hunger that is not uncommon among our contemporaries can be satisfied.

Second, the Church must find in our society today, alongside much that is corrupt and sinful, gospel values: the primacy of truth, the promotion of freedom, of human dignity and rights, of justice and peace, the protection of life and of the environment, concern for the poor and the disadvantaged. These are evidence of ideals, often promoted and initiated by non-Christians, upon which a better Europe can be built.

The new evangelization

Europe needs to be given a new soul and a new self-awareness. That is the magnitude of our task. In many ways the evangelization of Europe must be started all over again, as if it had never before taken place. If we think about this enormous task, we recognize that many things are required for effective evangelization. I will mention two. First, we need strong Christian communities, where those who seek God may go to pray and discover the secret of Christian life and action. Such centres may be religious houses, parish communities or any grouping of Christians assembled together in the name of Christ. Second, we need men and women, strong in faith and courage, to go out and preach the gospel where it is still unknown or, alas, has been once known and is now forgotten.

When two of the disciples of St John the Baptist followed Jesus, he asked them what they were looking for. They said: 'Rabbi, where are you staying?' He then gave his invitation: 'Come and see', he said (John 1.38,39). St Matthew records the command given to the apostles: 'Go, therefore, and make disciples of all nations, baptizing them in the name of the Father and of the Son and of the Holy Spirit' (Matt. 28.19). These two, the invitation to withdraw from the routine of daily life to be with Christ in prayer, and the command to go out and preach, are, in a remarkable way, symbolized by the patron saints of Europe: St Benedict, St Cyril and St Methodius.

St Benedict, the founder of Western monasticism, gathered around him people prepared to live in communities of prayer and faith. What gave meaning and significance to the lives of the monks was the daily praise and

worship of God. Around that every other activity re-
volved. Attention to God made them aware of their
duties to their neighbour and their stewardship of his
creation. They learned to cherish whatever was good,
noble and beautiful in human achievement. Although
withdrawn from the world, they created islands of genuine humanity in a sea of darkness and turmoil. Those
who lived there could say to the world, 'Come and see'.

Cyril and Methodius, though monks like Benedict,
went out to the peoples of their time. While Benedict was
essentially a community-builder, they were innovators,
missionaries. Faced with opposition and danger from
enemies outside and indeed inside the Church as well,
they sought by every means in their power to communicate directly to the people the revelation of Jesus Christ.
They translated the Scriptures into the language of the
people; they had to invent an alphabet in order to write
down a hitherto unrecorded language. They introduced
the vernacular into divine worship. 'Go therefore, and
make disciples of all nations.'

These three saints together witness to a number of
truths about the Church and about Europe. They remind
us, for example, that Europe has been shaped spiritually
and culturally by two currents of Christian tradition and
by two different but complementary cultures. St Benedict
is a key figure in the tradition which sprang from Rome.
Cyril and Methodius represent the contribution made by
Greece and by the Church of Constantinople. They are
patrons of the whole of Europe, witnessing to the Christianity which influenced the history of our continent,
shaped its institutions, formed its values.

Cyril and Methodius, in a special way, are models and
inspirations of ecumenism in Europe. When Pope John
Paul II proclaimed them patrons of Europe in 1980, he
linked that with what he called 'decisive steps in the
direction of full communion' between Orthodox and
Catholic Churches and with the dialogue initiated that

same year on the island of Patmos. The healing of that schism between East and West would be grace beyond compare for the People of God. It would give an almost irresistible impetus to the dialogue between Anglicans and Roman Catholics and would generate fresh enthusiasm for the task of reuniting Western Christianity. All three patron saints of Europe make it clear from their own diversity that the reuniting of Christianity need not involve the imposition of uniformity, but could, and should, involve due respect for other traditions, and liturgical practices.

Like Benedict, we have to put God into our lives, our activities, and concerns. We have to seek constantly the transcendent, plunge more deeply into the mystery that is God, and worship him more reverently. Like him we must establish and deepen community life. Like Cyril and Methodius we must refuse to be intimidated by opposition or oppression. We must seek every means of communicating freely with the peoples of today who, no matter under what political system they live, are starved of the word of truth and of the bread of life. We should be fearless innovators, speaking in the language of today and seeking by every means of modern mass communication to reach out to the people and speak to them of the Good News, which is the gospel of Jesus Christ. We must speak in particular to the young, who hold the future of our continent in their hands and who also are the Church of today and the hope of tomorrow.

When the young look today at Europe and at the Church, what do they see and what are they likely to think? Do they see only an ageing and disillusioned continent? Do they see a Church which they think has no message for the modern city and for the men and women of our day? Europe will rediscover its vitality and the Church its mission when the gospel is preached and lived in a manner which is both radical and relevant. The prophet Joel spoke of a time when 'your young men shall see visions and your old men shall dream dreams'. Let us share with the young our dreams.

For we dream of a Europe that will rediscover its faith and its unity; a Europe whose peoples will be free to inherit their own history and their own identity, true to their religion, their language and culture; a Europe prepared to live in peace and harmony, ready to solve quarrels by negotiation and not by armed might; a Europe which will protect all human life, respect human dignity, safeguard human rights; a Europe where family life will be fostered, individual liberties defended; a Europe where the hungry are fed, the weak cared for, the homeless sheltered; a continent whose peoples will stretch out their hands to the starving and the exploited.

We dream of a Church that will be intent on exploring the mystery that is God, a Church seeking to establish God's kingdom in the earthly city; a Church that will pray constantly, worship reverently, ponder the word of God and seek to reveal it to the world; a Church that is devoted to the pursuit of truth and to a deeper understanding of the teachings of Scripture and tradition; a Church true to its Lord, which seeks unity and reconciliation; a Church which is open house for all humanity, where the poor, the sinners, the weak, and the suffering can all find home and shelter. We dream of a Church which is faithful to its past, responsive to its present mission, and full of faith and hope for the future.

This is a vision of a Church and Europe that Benedict, Cyril and Methodius would have recognized and blessed. It can be our vision and inspiration.

A new beginning in Christ

For Christians, the birth of Christ always contains the promise of new beginnings. Christmas offers hope. He who is both God and man reveals not only the love of

God for humanity but also what humanity is meant to be and can become. It is for us to respond in faith and with courage. Then, during Lent and Easter, we prune so that the new life may blossom and bear fruit. We penetrate more deeply, and share more fully, the mystery of divine Love revealed in the death, resurrection and ascension of Jesus Christ. A good way to begin this is to recall the three temptations of Our Lord after his forty days of fasting and prayer. These temptations reveal the human condition. They tell us something about faith, hope, and the sovereignty of God over the whole creation.

First, the devil took advantage of Christ's hunger after forty days of fasting to tempt him to limit his concern to the relief of human need: give bread to the hungry, drink to the thirsty, clothe the naked, house the homeless. These are vital concerns. Our Father cares about them, but they cannot be the sole concern of the Saviour or of the Church which continues his mission. Men and women need daily bread. We need too a reason for living, a sense of purpose, a vision. We need the bread of life, the word of truth which comes from God. The best gift to the world is the revelation of God in Jesus Christ.

The second temptation was to seek a sign from the Father, a dramatic intervention to overwhelm all disbelief and opposition. On Calvary there was an echo of the same temptation: 'If you are the Son of God, come down from the Cross and we will believe.' But miraculous escape is a delusion. The children of God have to be prepared to wait in faith and enduring hope. We realize, like Christ, that love alone will conquer hate and that life is found only in the experience of death. In the darkness we have faith in the light, we hope for life without end. Despair paralyses the human will. Instead we offer the inspiration of hope and new life.

The final temptation is to use earthly power and strength to compel the good we wish to achieve. Whatever our motive we must follow the path God the Father has shown us in the life of his Son. In faith and hope we must be content with weakness and apparent failure. The blessing we bring to our world is the message of Jesus Christ that we must communicate and put into practice. It is the only answer to the unbelief and moral anarchy which causes so much misery. It is our task to witness to the truth and commit ourselves to the gospel of reconciliation, peace, unity, and love of others. We must be consistent and whole-hearted in our service of God.

ONE

Peace amid thorns

In the frontispiece to the old Benedictine Breviary, the words *Pax inter spinas* were encircled by a crown of thorns. The symbolism and meaning are clear. Prayer, worship, union with God create for us that peace which the world cannot give and which is achieved by grace and not by our own efforts. In the midst of pain and suffering there can be a serenity and even joy which has nothing to do with indifference or stoicism. It is rooted in the conviction that all is created and sustained by the love of God our Father and by faith that in the words of Julian of Norwich 'all will be well and all manner of things will be well'.

Perhaps we can begin to understand what this conviction and faith really mean by asking what difference they make in practice. Is it possible, for instance, to detect any difference between, say, an International Red Cross worker and one from Trocaire, Caritas, or our English and Welsh CAFOD? Is their motivation the same? Do their priorities differ? Are both in fact expressing the same humanitarian concern but using different language? In all areas of social concern believers, agnostics, and even atheists certainly can work with admirable commitment on similar projects and are valued and trusted collaborators. Believers, however, have, or should have, a unified and coherent approach to life of which their compassion is but part. For them, as for us, the life we share in Jesus Christ and the truth which he revealed and by which we live should unify every aspect of our existence. It means that the same values underlie personal, public and international attitudes and that under no circumstances may we simply shrug our shoulders, admit to 'compassion fatigue', and turn our backs on any human need.

One of the commonest misunderstandings among people is to imagine that life can somehow be divided up into separate sealed compartments. It is commonly believed in today's secular society that individuals are free to choose their own values and standards of morality, which remain their private concern and are just as valid as all others. In society, as a result of this philosophy, shared values no longer underpin public policy. Expediency and the will of the majority determine that. International relationships are forged and maintained purely on perceived national interests. This is the reason for the sometimes glaring discrepancy, alien to the true believer, between personal convictions and public behaviour, and explains the frequently selfish and short-sighted behaviour of so-called Christian nations on the world stage.

True Christians should be immediately recognizable and distinctive. They should be fundamentally humble and joyous in accepting the reality of creation, the mystery of the incarnation and redemption, and the consequent transformation and sanctification of all that exists. This threefold affirmation of creation, redemption, and sanctification corresponds to the way we see the Trinity at work among us—as God the Father and Creator, as God the

Son made man for us and Saviour of the world, and as
God the Holy Spirit, whose life and love poured out
into creation continue to reconcile, unite and lift back
to God all that is. The role of believers, then, is essentially to play our part in making real and present in our
world the purposes and power of the Triune God. It is
his work, not ours, and so we have every ground for
peace and confidence in all that we undertake in his
name. It means also that the same golden thread runs
through our individual spirituality, our community concerns, and our commitment to world peace and
development.

Blessed are the peacemakers

We need to begin, as always, from where we are, our
inmost selves, our human condition. It is important to
realize that we experience in our lives the same pressures
and responses which are so vividly portrayed in the
gospels. It is also important to see that the life, death,
and resurrection of Christ is both mystery and supreme
sacrament. In him and through him our individual lives
are given meaning and eternal value.

As we reflect on the gospel story, most of us easily
identify, I think, with Peter that morning in his boat
when at the Lord's bidding after a fruitless night's fishing
he had netted an amazing catch: 'Depart from me, for I
am a sinful man.' Brought face to face with the power
and goodness of God, we experience too clearly our own
selfishness and failure. Disturbed by the challenge of our
calling by Christ we may at first prefer to be left alone.
But then the gospels are also full of those in desperate
need seeking relief for both body and soul. The lepers,
the blind beggar on the road to Jericho, the paralysed,
the lame, the woman suffering the issue of blood who
sought only to touch the hem of his garment, even those

who were beyond all human help (like the widow's son at Naim, Jairus' daughter and Lazarus), all found in Jesus health, wholeness, liberation from sin, and abundance of new life.

In our own case we know only too well that flight from God is no answer. We may be frequently downcast at the evidence of our own mistakes and weakness, but the proper response is not to hide from the justice of God but to throw ourselves onto his mercy and compassion. Only those ready to admit their need of help will ever find it. Until we are brought face to face with the truth of our condition we are unable to accept salvation and a saviour.

No one of us is ever entirely blameless. We may not be guilty of positive wrongdoing, but our sins of omission, our lack of genuine love, damage, and ultimately can destroy us. If you think back to that picture of the Last Judgement in chapter 25 of St Matthew's Gospel, those condemned were the people who had failed to feed the hungry, give drink to the thirsty, clothe the naked, visit the sick and imprisoned. They had not been guilty of injustice but of a neglect that contributed to the misery of others. That in itself is enough to condemn them as it may condemn us.

Sins of omission require more than forgiveness. They demand from us a positive response to the gospel of love and solidarity. That response will not come from our human will, power, and resources but is itself a gift of God or, more precisely, the love of God alive and active through us and in us. We are called to be channels of that love, but first we must accept Jesus Christ as our saviour and the source of that love.

This is the beginning of our quest for wholeness and holiness; it sets our feet on the paths of peace. Conscious of our personal limitations, our failures and our omissions, we can still experience an inner peace once we realize that we are not the centre and purpose of creation, but that we exist for something and someone greater than ourselves.

This is a practical and personal acceptance of the truth of creation. All things are made through and in the Word of God; they are a limited but real reflection of God himself. We have to see not only our own intrinsic goodness and loveableness but to accept this as gift of God. And to recognize that same goodness and loveableness in other humans and in all that God has made.

A revolution then occurs in the way we look at life. If all is gift and reflection of God, then it is our privilege and duty to maintain that harmony, balance, and right order in creation which stem directly from God. As rational beings, we alone can detect the mind of God and correct failures in realizing his plan. Our creativity, technology, and work reflect and to some extent share God's endless outpouring of creation.

We should begin to appreciate that in all things we are sustained and surrounded by the love of God in creation and this makes for peace. In secular and economic attitudes, individuals are nowadays encouraged to see themselves as essentially consumers and producers and in competition with others. In a cut-throat and hostile world it is every man for himself and the Devil take the hindmost.

In fact, many people need enemies for their own sense of identity. They are defined as much by what they oppose as by what they support. Conflict and confrontation characterize much of our politics, industrial relations, and international affairs. Because of the way we have learned to think it is often easier to mobilize people to oppose than to co-operate. Hostility, anger, and envy of others intensify. Those, however, who see themselves as children of God and as part of a single creation have to reject such attitudes and their destructive consequences. They develop partnership not conflict, friendship not hostility, peace not war.

The inner peace and harmony which an individual enjoys as the result of a true understanding of creation are transfigured by an awareness of incarnation and redemption. The birth of Jesus as true God and true man was the fulfilment of the promises and prophecies of the Old Testament. In a manner beyond all human expectation and understanding the presence and power of God has entered our human history and changed it for ever. Two thousand years ago Christ lived and died as an outcast in torment on Calvary, and yet in and through his suffering and death he freed us from sin and banished once and for all the curse of death. Since then individuals have been able, through faith and the sacraments, to be part of that mystery of redemption, filling up in their flesh what is lacking in Christ's suffering for the sake of his body (Col. 1.24). In a very real sense, the passion of Christ continues and will continue to the end of time whenever his brothers and sisters suffer. 'I was hungry and you gave me no food . . .' If we enter fully and with faith into the pain, the rejection and the frustrations of our own situation, we can find in the midst of the pain the peace that Our Lord and Master never lost and now shares with us. Both the pain and the peace are part of the continuing mystery of the redemption. Through them we are each made holy and grow in the life and love of God.

The same symbolism of peace amid the thorns is equally relevant when we turn from the individual to the community and begin to consider what should be our Christian response as a community to suffering on a global level. How can such suffering be reconciled with our belief in an all-loving God and Father? How can we maintain the peace of God in our hearts when we confront the pain of our brothers and sisters?

The first thing to be said is that God never directly wills what is negative and destructive. Suffering and death are in large measure the result of human stupidity, sinfulness, and aggression. Natural disasters are explicable by the sequence of cause and effect; they could be averted only by the repeated miraculous intervention of God. Human beings are meant to employ every resource to prevent, control, and perhaps even largely eliminate much suffering from our world. You know the prayer that is frequently reproduced: 'Lord grant me the serenity to accept the things I cannot change; courage to change the things I can, and wisdom to know the difference.'

Before I embark on projects to change the world I need to be clear in my own mind why and how I should be acting and what chance of success I have. Then I need all the courage and determination in the world if I am to effect change.

Catholic social teaching

It is here that Christ, the light of the peoples, is our guide in our approach to all the problems of politics, development, and the care of our planet. Faithful to his teaching the Church has, especially in this century, fashioned a social doctrine which has been called one of the Church's best-kept secrets. As well as the Second Vatican Council and that seminal and prophetic document *Gaudium et Spes*, the Popes have addressed to the Church and the world a series of encyclicals of quite remarkable power and insight. In the early 1960s Pope John XXIII wrote 'Christianity and Social Progress' (*Mater et Magistra*) and 'Peace on Earth' (*Pacem in Terris*); Pope Paul VI followed with the 'Development of People' (*Populorum Progressio*) in 1967, while the present Pope has written a trio of encyclicals on social issues: 'On Human Work' (*Laborem Exercens*) in 1981; 'On Social Concerns' (*Sollicitudo Rei Socialis*) in 1987 and 'The Hundredth Anniversary of Rerum Novarum' (*Centesimus Annus*) in 1991.

The canvas is vast and I want to emphasize no more

than four key words which, I suggest, help us to approach the world's problems and pain and to preserve at the same time the peace in our hearts which the world cannot give. The four words are *dignity*, *development*, *solidarity*, and *subsidiarity*. I can do no more than hint at the power and richness contained in each concept, and urge you to read or reread both the Second Vatican Council and the social encyclicals. However, because of its relevance to the present state of Europe, I shall develop the notion of solidarity in the following chapters.

The theme of *human dignity* is fundamental to the Church's teaching. There are grounds for saying that the principal contribution the Church makes to society today is its unswerving commitment to human dignity and rights. That commitment is based on the biblical understanding that each human being is made in the image and likeness of God. He gives each individual a dignity that nothing can eradicate, and entitles each to unconditional respect. No single person may ever be sacrificed for the sake of some alleged greater good or in the name of some principle, however exalted.

Individuals are to be valued independently of their usefulness to society, their productivity or lack of it, the quality of life they enjoy or can expect in the future.

That dignity is further enhanced if the individual becomes a new creation in Christ. Then that person is reborn with a supernatural life that comes from God alone and is destined to share the very life and love of God both here and hereafter. That creates relationships within the Body of Christ which go far beyond the ties of flesh and blood which human kinship create. There is then created the *koinonia* and fellowship which surpass all other human groupings. This has consequences when we come to reflect later on solidarity.

It is surely clear that this acceptance of the dignity of each human being must result in practical approaches to political issues and international relations. It must outlaw discrimination of all kinds, whether based on race, colour, culture, religion, or gender. It must argue for the greatest possible equality in the eyes of the law, in employment, in financial rewards for equal effort and skill, and in educational and training opportunities.

There has to be absolute respect for each person's human rights, principally of course for the right to life, now so seriously and systematically threatened by genetic engineering, abortion, and euthanasia. Other rights about freedom of religion, the quality of life, the right to education, housing, work and a living wage, justice, marriage and family are all consequent upon the right to life. They are however important in creating a society and environment that protects and fosters men and women throughout life. Our concern must be for every stage of human life from conception to our return to God.

All notions of racial superiority, of imperialism, of systematic domination and exploitation of others must surely wither and die. Christians who truly recognize the divine image in themselves and in others are radically and irreversibly changed. For one thing, they can never again be thoroughgoing individualists or indifferent to relationships. That is because the God of whom we are the image is not a solitary, but a Trinitarian God, not strictly an I, but a We: Father, Son and Holy Spirit. Our inner reality bears the imprint of the Triune God and is essentially the endless act of loving and being loved, of knowing and being known by the three persons in one God. It is inevitable and necessary, then, that we, as humans, are essentially people who relate to each other and form community.

From that social character of humanity flow, I believe, the allied principles of solidarity and subsidiarity, concepts which through Catholic social teaching, have entered into European political thinking and language. *Solidarity* recognizes a community of interests between all nations on this single planet. Pope Paul VI in *Populorum Progressio* spelled this out with deep conviction in 1967:

> There can be no progress towards the single development of man without the simultaneous development of all humanity in the spirit of solidarity. This duty is the concern of the better-off nations. Their obligation stems from a brotherhood that is at once human and supernatural and takes on a threefold aspect:
> - the duty of human solidarity—the aid that the rich nations must give to developing countries;
> - the duty of social justice—the rectification of inequitable trade relations between powerful nations and weak nations;
> - the duty of universal charity—the effort to bring about a world that is more human towards all persons, where all will be able to give and receive without one group making progress at the expense of the other. The question is urgent for on it depends the future of the civilization of the world.
> (PP 43, 44)

Solidarity is, in the Pope's words, both human and supernatural. The fundamental and religious respect for human dignity which characterizes it also leads into the principle of *subsidiarity*. This is also about much more than decentralization and local responsibility. It is a recognition that people, because of who and what they are, should be empowered to take decisions for their own lives with due regard for the interests of the wider community. It is clearly opposed to excessive bureaucracy, to paternalism, to the imposition of policies and strategies by the strong on the weak. It emphasizes the need to develop human potential as God-given and as the greatest resource possessed by this planet.

Development is, then, much more than providing the possibility for economic progress and self-sufficiency. It must embrace the whole spectrum of human needs and potential. It is a spiritual as well as a political activity.

In his message for Lent 1992, Pope John Paul II declared that all 'without exception' are called to share the table of creation. He said that the Church 'in more recent times has repeatedly preached the universal destination of the goods of creation, both material and spiritual, as a central theme of her social teaching'. He goes on to say that the encyclical *Centesimus Annus* 'is meant to encourage reflection on this universal destination of goods, which comes before all particular forms of private property and which should give them their true meaning'.

The Church's commitment to development and our sharing in it is not a response of charity but of justice. It flows directly from our understanding of the meaning of life and of our human destiny. As Pope Paul VI taught in *Populorum Progressio*:

> The Bible, from the first page on, teaches us that the whole of creation is for man, that it is his responsibility to develop it by intelligent effort, and by means of his labour to perfect it, so to speak, for his use ... Each man has therefore the right to find in the world what is necessary for himself. The recent Council reminded us of this: 'God intended the earth and all it contains for the use of all men and peoples, so created goods should flow fairly to all, regulated by justice and accompanied by charity' (*Gaudium et Spes* 69). (PP 22)

The demands of justice are at the heart of the Gospel. I quote the words of the 1971 Synod of Bishops:

> Action on behalf of justice and participation in the transformation of the world fully appear to us as a constitutive dimension of the preaching of the Gospel, or, in other words, of the Church's mission for the redemption of the human race and its

liberation from every oppressive situation. ('Justice in the World', Introduction)

Here, I think, we need to create within the Catholic communities of Europe a new awareness. They have been brought up in a tradition of almsgiving and voluntary aid. They need to open their eyes to a broader horizon. We all need to reflect on our human solidarity within Europe and outside. We need to see the unbreakable connection between love of God and love of our neighbour. As with peace and war, the difficulties seem insurmountable. The world's anarchy and greed seem unconquerable. The Christian can never despair and never retreat from the world, leaving it to its own devices. We go forward hoping in Christ: 'because God wanted all perfection to be found in him and all things to be reconciled through him and for him, everything in heaven and everything on earth, when he made peace by his death on the cross' (Col. 1.19–20).

Inner peace and harmony and the peace, tranquillity, and good order of communities and society are guaranteed only when the reality of God's creation is respected and accepted. In the midst of thorns—whether they be personal sufferings and frustrations, or the immense injustices and deprivations of our world—it is possible to find God and to allow ourselves to be channels of his peace. Our commitments to charity and aid work, to world peace, is not a response of pity, or even of compassion, but much more a realization that this is the response we must make in justice to the sinful mess that men and women have made of our society and our world. It is for us, working with God as co-creators in his world, to give his life and love fuller expression in ourselves and in others. In him is our peace.

TWO

Solidarity and morals

On the agenda of a religious leaders meeting at Lambeth Palace in 1993 were three words: morality, racism, and the family. As I began to reflect with a view to making my contribution to the discussions, I came across the following text from the medieval Jewish commentator, Rashi, on Deuteronomy 32, with a commentary on it by Bernard Marauni. This is what I read:

'God is led to show his love towards Israel in the same way as the eagle which is full of tenderness for its little ones; the eagle does not enter its nest brutally, but first beats and flaps its wings above the nest so that the eaglets wake up and have the strength to welcome it. The eagle flies over its little ones; without pressing heavily upon them it glides, touching them and not touching them.' The *tohu wabohu*, the separation between the waters above and below (which prefigures the separation between heaven and earth) manifests this distance that the

Creator puts between himself and his creation in order to safeguard its autonomy. Without it, the world would be 'overwhelmed' by the divine, absorbed into it: the *tohu wabohu* resides in creation, since through it the world distinguishes itself from the divine and gives itself a place as creature. However, its distance from the Creator should not be understood as an absolute separation, since that would detach the world radically from the Creator. In fact it is only virtual and paradoxical. It is 'supposed' and cannot be thought.[1]

'The eagle flies over its little ones; without pressing heavily upon them it glides, touching them and not touching them.' This image of the eagle hovering above the nest is a beautiful one. The transcendence and majesty of God does not impose, does not smother us, but invites and beckons us to open our hearts and to feed on his love.

This image provides a way of thinking about human freedom which does justice to a sense of autonomy on the one hand and of dependence on the other. I would like to explore some aspects of this freedom, as it relates especially to spirituality, to morality, and to solidarity. The issues of racism and family life find their right context within these three.

The law of perfect freedom

Freedom is a priceless gift bestowed by God. Perhaps the most fundamental freedom we possess is that of choosing how we respond to God's love. It is freedom to explore a reality infinitely greater and more wonderful than we can ever imagine. Now love cannot be forced or coerced. It is of its essence a free choice. Having the capacity to love means we can choose not to. The eagle hovers, but does not overwhelm the eaglets. Furthermore, to be able to respond to the love of God by loving in return presupposes a certain distance between us and God.

The existence of God is not obvious. The revelation of God in human history and in individual human lives is not always so transparent as to compel us to acknowledge his sovereignty and dominion over us. So we have to choose to bridge the distance that separates us from God, or, more strictly speaking, choose to respond to the initiatives which God takes to meet us where we are, that is in the reality of our daily lives.

'The eagle flies over its little ones; without pressing heavily upon them it glides, touching them and not touching them.' Now the experience of being touched by God can take many forms. The most direct we call mystical experience, a frightening word, no doubt, but one that describes a knowing and a desiring of God which has no other explanation but his action in our souls. It is more common than is often realized. There is also a yearning to seek a meaning and purpose to human life; the sense that the universe cannot explain either its own existence or its intelligibility; the awareness of moral obligation, of goodness, of beauty, and of truth—these are some of the reasons that lead us to look beyond ourselves and our world, to One who can satisfy both an intellectual search for ultimate truth and a spiritual and emotional longing for love. In his book *Real Presences*, George Steiner remarks how he fears there are now many people for whom the existence of God is no longer a real question, as they have no language or religious symbolism in which the possibility can even be contemplated.[2] I do not, myself, take such a pessimistic view. It seems to me that there are always hints and echoes of the divine which whisper to us and invite us to respond, for God is ever at work in human hearts. There is, however, a real need for those of us who believe in the God of Abraham, Isaac, and Jacob to articulate that belief in a way which

shows it to be appealing, and in a language which con-
nects with the experiences of the many people in our
society for whom the Judaeo-Christian tradition is now
largely alien. The eagle has not abandoned the nest but
hovers, touching and not touching, coaxing us gently,
individually and collectively, to respond with love, while
always respecting our freedom.

Why is the existence of God not more obvious? One
answer might be that it requires the deep engagement of
the whole person before the question of God becomes
real. What is obvious requires no engagement, no reflection, no struggle. To go in search of God, on the other
hand, requires effort, and a measure of self-discipline and
self-denial. The voice of God does not speak dramatically,
as in a hurricane or an earthquake or a fire but calls to
us gently in the very depths of our being. To hear the
voice of God demands some solitude, silence, and stillness. In our society today there is too much noise, both
around and within us, and the quiet voice of God becomes
stifled. But in a moment of gentle stillness, God not only
reveals something of himself but he transforms us too. For
if God exists, it is the most fundamental truth of all. It
changes everything. It cannot both be true and not
matter.

This involvement with the question of God has, of
course, to be a personal quest. No one can undertake it
for another. The discovery of God is always unique
too, for it is no less than the touch of the eagle awakening us, and bringing us to recognize that we are in a
relationship of dependence, of love bestowed and love
returned. God is hidden only because, as T. S. Eliot
put it so well, 'human kind cannot bear very much
reality'.[3]

To see the religious quest as the pursuit of the real is, I
believe, of great importance. There is ultimately no opposition between religion and life: the true conflict is between
what is real and what is illusory. Genuine religious faith

leads to a fuller and richer human life, not a suppression of it. The truth sets us free.

Are the moral requirements of the Scriptures—the life of the Commandments—an imposition, a constraint upon human freedom? Genuine human freedom, it is argued, requires us to determine our own moral codes, not submit to those of others. The image of the eagle comes back to me as I reflect now on moral freedom. We have to recognize both a due autonomy, and a real dependence.

Morality presupposes freedom. Unless I can genuinely choose, and unless I have some knowledge or awareness of what it is I am choosing, I cannot be held morally responsible for my actions. Morality presupposes a basic moral awareness, that good should be done and evil avoided. The crucial issue—and it is of real practical import in society today—is: who decides 'the good'?

I was very much struck by the following exchange reported in the *Tablet* between a teacher and his students in America. A hypothetical moral dilemma faced by a young woman was put before the students. The teacher asked them what she should do. The response was 'It's her choice.' The teacher insisted, 'Yes. But how should she choose? And on what grounds?' The students replied again: 'It's her choice.' In fact the students were making a moral claim. They were saying that there is no value more precious than that a person should be free to determine his or her own good. On this view there can be no moral argument, because each of us creates our own moral rules; and in the name of tolerance we should refrain from moral judgement, as this would be to impose our rules on others.

Here is freedom cut loose from its bearings. The freedom to choose is extended to deciding what is good and what is evil. We cannot do this without denying the fundamental nature of humanity. For the defining features of human nature do not change, and they generate certain universal and permanent requirements of human well-being and fulfilment which moral norms seek to express. The search for the good is nothing other than the pursuit of the truly human. We are guided on this search in two ways. First, there is rooted in humanity a God-given impulse towards moral integrity and goodness, unless, of course, that impulse has been stifled. It can be. Second, there are divinely revealed commandments which are of universal and abiding application.

In our society there are, of course, still some widely held moral standards. Basic values such as honesty, kindness, generosity, consideration for others, compassion, faithfulness in relationships, and respect for human life are shared by very many people. The real difficulty is that there is a loss of confidence that these virtues are always essential if human beings are to flourish; and there is often a denial that there are objective moral norms which are more than expressions of personal opinion.

The image of the eagle hovering above the nest gave us a sense of autonomy and yet also of dependence. What we are witnessing in our society is an over-emphasis on autonomy, and a denial of dependence. But what is left of moral freedom if God has revealed the good to us? Are we not reduced to total dependency? Is there not an opposite danger to unbridled autonomy, namely an unthinking and uncritical compliance with an external moral law? In his recent encyclical on morality, *Veritatis Splendor*, the Pope quotes Psalm 1, 'Blessed is the man who takes delight in the law of the Lord', and goes on:

> Patterned on God's freedom, man's freedom is not negated by his obedience to the divine law; indeed, only through this obedience does it abide in the truth and conform to human dignity. This is clearly stated by the [Second Vatican] Council: 'Human dignity requires man to act through conscious and free choice, as motivated and prompted personally

from within, and not through blind internal impulse
or merely external pressure. Man achieves such
dignity when he frees himself from all subservience
to his feelings, and in a free choice of the good,
pursues his own end by effectively and assiduously
marshalling the appropriate means' (*Gaudium et
Spes* 17). (VS 42)

Moral responsibility, then, requires each of us to exercise our own judgement. The eagle hovers, but does not
land. We are not left orphans. We are guided, but God
does not decide for us. We cannot escape from the
dignity of responsibility through blind or unthinking
obedience. In the muddle and complexity of many practical situations we are entrusted with the responsibility of
moral choice. This is the hinterland of moral freedom.
Our part is to use the gift of that freedom by always
seeking to choose wisely and well, in conformity with
objective moral norms.

What kind of solidarity?

Freedom, then, has to recognize its own limitations. It
has to be balanced by an awareness of other values. A
crucial one is *solidarity*. Solidarity has been defined as
the ability and openness of a person to share the resources
necessary for life, even when they are limited. Among
those resources should be included access to food, housing, work, education, and other basic human rights and
freedoms. To live in solidarity, in other words, is to
acknowledge that other people matter.

The eagle flies over a single nest. Humanity is one.
Each of us was born into a family, into a community,
and into the single human family. These are not associations we chose to join. We are members whether we like
it or not. The Scriptures teach us that God created us all

in his image and likeness, as brothers and sisters, as a single community. We are a part of, and interdependent with, the rest of creation.

The idea of a common humanity can sound utopian, particularly when we reflect that in practice solidarity seems to presuppose some limits. Human communities of all kinds, after all, seem to be defined by the fact that some are included in them while others are left out. In fact there are many limited solidarities: family, village, town, region, nation, European, but none of these need exclude the others, and more important still, none should be turned into a false absolute. It is when people begin to define their identity as human beings solely and exclusively in terms of membership of a class, an ethnic group, a nation, or even a religion, that solidarity can become a force for evil rather than for good. And even as I write, the barbarism in Bosnia continues, with people killing each other indiscriminately for no better reason than their being from a different religious or ethnic background.

In all parts of Europe there is a disturbing rise in racism, xenophobia, and anti-Semitism which has to be deplored and condemned. These are ugly manifestations of a sickness of soul which urgently needs to be healed.

The desire to stigmatize others, to exclude and to scapegoat them stems at root from fear. The stranger, the outcast, is victimized as a way of compensating for a lack of security, a fear of losing a distinctive group or national identity. And an unreal fantasy about the goodness and virtue of that identity is fed by imputing to those excluded or victimized all the blame for its failure. This is the warped and evil logic of the Holocaust, and of ethnic cleansing in Bosnia today. The temptation to succumb to it lies with us all.

Of course, there can be reasonable and well-founded fears, for instance of natural dangers such as environmental pollution, or of belligerent and unscrupulous political regimes. These rightly generate a solidarity among those seeking to meet them. But the kind of fear that leads to the expulsion of immigrants, to racial violence, or to ethnic cleansing is of a different character. It is irrational and generalized.

The only antidote to this fear is love. The Scriptures teach us that God always remains faithful to Israel. Despite our sin, God is unfailing in his love. And our acceptance of that love, that we matter to God, allows us to face our real selves and to acknowledge our failings. We can begin to acknowledge the worst in ourselves, because the truth is ultimately friendly. As the Psalmist writes, 'Yahweh is my light and my salvation, whom shall I fear?' (Ps. 27.1). Once we can accept ourselves, we can more easily accept others, and respect their value.

In fact, the acceptance of God's unconditional love for each person leads us to see that human solidarity has to be universal. The eagle hovers over the nest, and tends to the eaglets, loving them each and caring for all. Each person has an absolute and unique value simply as a human being, and not through membership of any more limited group. To each is due respect, for all are made in the image and likeness of God. Local loyalties are important, but must always be balanced by a wider loyalty to those beyond their borders.

And it is perhaps more helpful to think of this wider solidarity not as a lofty ideal, but as obliging us all to be in solidarity with whoever comes our way, with the one whom we have to face in a situation, or with whom we are confronted. In very practical ways, we are all on a personal and a political level constantly given opportunities for building up this genuine solidarity.

At the political level there are some striking examples at the present time of such opportunities. I think of the progress which has been made in South Africa. Here is an astonishing example of the closed and evil solidarity of apartheid slowly and painfully giving way to a vision of a more open and inclusive solidarity, a community which would embrace all South Africans. We must all pray that a lasting peace, founded on justice, may yet come to that troubled land.

Another example is provided by the remarkable accord reached between the PLO and the Israeli Government. Whatever view one takes of the specific terms of their agreement—and I am not in a position to make a judgement—the fact remains that these two old adversaries have been able to reach an agreement which recognizes certain rights of both Israelis and Palestinians in some areas. Without doubt the eventual outcome is still far from certain. But the accord itself symbolizes the waning of entrenched enmity and confrontation, and opens a window to a distant vision of a future peaceful co-existence.

A third example is Northern Ireland. So far no peace proposal has even been put forward. Yet recently a number of developments, including a groundswell of popular feeling in both communities and some apparent shifts within republican terrorist groups, have led many competent and knowledgeable people to speak of the best opportunity for peace in the province in twenty-five years.

The tragic history of Northern Ireland illustrates all too well the dangers of false absolutes, of an exclusive solidarity, and, sadly, of the ambiguous role which religion can play in generating fear, rather than love. What seems to be more widely and deeply accepted by those in Britain and Ireland involved in seeking a political solution now is that no settlement can work which does not have the consent of both communities in Northern Ireland, and allows them both to feel at home. The development of greater mutual respect, of confidence and of a willingness to make sacrifices for the sake of a greater good is increasingly seen as essential. Again, we should pray for the success of the efforts of those in authority who are seeking to encourage an open solidarity between the communities in Northern Ireland, based on the growth of mutual trust.

These three examples of South Africa, Israel, and the PLO, and Northern Ireland illustrate both the apparent intractability of human sin and failure, and also the possibilities for transformation which lie even within them.

As European peoples and governments continue to grapple with the aftermath of the collapse of Communism, persistent economic difficulties, and an uncertain and precarious outlook, the temptation everywhere seems to be the pursuit of narrow national or sectional interests. The moral requirement of acting in solidarity demands that such interests are not pursued at the cost of the welfare of others. At a time of fear and uncertainty it behoves all in public office to resist racism and always to avoid stirring up irrational fears for political ends; it is incumbent on us all to do what we can for those in real need who seek our help. There should, for instance, be no question of withdrawing humanitarian assistance from Bosnia as long as it can still be delivered.

These points illustrate that moral considerations cannot and should not be excluded from political life or the conduct of international affairs. Solidarity, in public affairs as in personal ones, acts as a check on the exercise of freedom, recalling us to the fact that we all inhabit the same world and share a common humanity. We have a duty to respect the dignity of all those who cross our path, do to all we can to break down the barriers of ignorance, prejudice, and distrust which divide people and cause so much suffering.

I have strayed a little from the image I started with, of the eagle and the nest, but all I have been speaking of is the restoration of a peace and harmony in the world, which only becomes possible when people are able to see both autonomy and dependence in their true context. To accept that people matter, that human beings have an intrinsic worth and dignity, is much easier said than done. If it were tried out more in practice, even marginally, the world would be transformed.

The image of the eagle and the nest is, of course, the image of a family. This is the archetypal human experience, and the root of all I have been saying. Solidarity calls us all to be brothers and sisters, but unless we have some prior experience of family life and security it is difficult to grasp what this entails.

The family is the school in which we learn the art of living. In family life we grow from the total dependency of childhood to the autonomy of adult life. In the family we learn to love by first being loved and accepted. Morality is learned not only by teaching but by doing, and by the example of parents. In the family we learn the difference between right and wrong, the importance of self-discipline, kindness, and faithfulness in relationships. The well-being of the family, as much as any other factor, holds the key to the future.

The eagle hovers over the eaglets, touching and not touching, awakening them to freedom. True freedom, for which we all yearn, does not come from rejecting the dependence with which we are born. The most precious and basic human experience is to be loved and accepted by a parent. At a deep level we carry and treasure this through life. And it is also the most profound religious truth, that we are loved, unconditionally, by God. A total acceptance of this in our hearts transforms and heals us. It enables us to recognize our utter dependence on him, and our interdependence with the rest of humanity. Then we can learn to fly, free of the nest, in real freedom and solidarity with others, yet always guided by a loving presence whom we acknowledge and worship as being at once our origin and our destiny.

Notes

1. *Midrash Rabba I, Genesis Rabba*, Commentary by Bernard Marauni, *Bereshit* V (Paris, 1987), quoted by Christian Duquoc in *Concilium*, August 1992, p. 9.
2. George Steiner, *Real Presences: Is There Anything in What We Say?*, Faber and Faber, 1991.
3. 'Burnt Norton', *Collected Poems 1909–1962*, Faber and Faber, 1963, p. 190.

Solidarity and freedom

Pentecost is now. The Spirit is constantly at work in the Church and in the world, and to live in the movement of the Spirit is to expect renewal and transformation; it is to believe in the future, trusting in him whose hands sustain all creation in being and whose breath gives life to all creatures. The book of Wisdom teaches us that 'The Spirit of the Lord, indeed, fills the whole world' (Wis. 1.7). Our attitude to the modern world, therefore, must never be one of rejection motivated by fear. Human failure and wickedness can never extinguish or ultimately defeat the loving power of God who has created and sustains all things in being. We must strive to see our world and its peoples with respect and love, eager to play our part, here and now, in building the Kingdom of God.

The profound consequences of the revolutions in Central and Eastern Europe will take generations to emerge and unfold. We are still only now just beginning to grasp the extent of the social, political, economic, and spiritual implications for Europe and the wider world. A profound *metanoia* is called for, and this leads me to further reflect on the themes of freedom and solidarity. These two profound ideas belong and fit together: they contain vital and balancing truths about the nature of humanity and our common destiny. They can greatly help us in seeking to understand more deeply the cultural forces shaping European societies today.

Both freedom and solidarity find their source and inspiration in Christ, 'in whom all things were made' (John 1.3). For true freedom is the possibility, realized through the death and resurrection of Christ, of our responding to his call to love God and our neighbour. We are always free to say 'Here I am'; we are never coerced. Freedom, then, is the responsibility given to us to make choices. It is a gift, and, like all gifts, it can be misused.

Solidarity is the practical expression in the world of the communion between God and humanity made possible through the death and resurrection of Christ. The Church exists as the source and sign of this communion. The mystery of the Church is a participation in the Trinitarian life of God. This sharing in the one divine reality is the basis for communion in the Church and so for solidarity in the world. Thus solidarity is the recognition of the communion of the single human family into which we are all born. From this follows our responsibility to share with others the goods of creation, which are meant for all. The Holy Father in *Sollicitudo Rei Socialis* stresses that solidarity,

> is not a feeling of vague compassion or shallow distress at the misfortunes of so many people, both near and far. On the contrary, it is a firm and persevering determination to commit oneself to the common good; that is to say to the good of all and of each individual, because we are all really responsible for all. (SRS 38)

True solidarity flows from a realization that all creation

forms a single whole and that human persons are interdependent both with one another, and with the rest of creation. To accept our solidarity is to acknowledge that we have no absolute ownership of anything. All that we have, including our lives, is given to us on trust for the benefit of all.

It is clear immediately that this understanding of freedom and solidarity is contrary to much that is said and done in modern European societies. Indeed, we might even say that Communist Europe abused solidarity and denied freedom, while Western Europe has abused freedom and, in part, denied solidarity. This may be an oversimplification, but there is some truth in it nevertheless.

The legacy of Communism

Communism was the systematic and grotesque parody of solidarity with its ideal of the common good. It promoted an atheistic, materialist and revolutionary ideal of human community and interdependence. It ruthlessly subjected human freedom to the will of a few powerful individuals in the name of the State. It denied the value of anything higher than the commune. The human person was seen as essentially the 'product of society' with no ultimate or transcendent value. Moreover, creation was treated with no respect, as is now all too clear in the appalling legacy of environmental degradation and pollution in post-Communist countries.

Communism had no soul and it rotted from the inside. What finally collapsed in 1989 was the shell of a creature long since dead. The defeat of Communism by largely peaceful protest was a triumph of humanity over inhumanity, of the Spirit of Truth over the lies of the State. It was a victory for the power of love over the love of power, and surely one of the most providential events in human history.

But the legacy of Communism is with us still, and in even deeper ways than environmental destruction. For the damage done to the human spirit through persecution and systematic oppression is incalculable. If human beings can oppress one another in this way for so long, what are we? Let me quote from Jósef Tischner, Professor of Christian Philosophy at the Papal Institute in Krakow:

> If after the Enlightenment people asked how it was still at all possible to believe in God; after these immense crimes of communism one wonders whether and how it will ever be possible again to rely on man. Doubt in man was a significant factor in the destruction of social bonds and finally undermined communism itself. And today this doubt is the greatest hindrance in the search for a way to democracy. The communist disease in the post-communist era is based on calling man totally into question—doubt is all-embracing.[1]

Many in post-Communist Europe have turned to the churches in the aftermath of Communism, painfully aware that a demoralization of the human person has taken place which urgently needs to be reversed. Although I have no direct experience, I can imagine that, given the way the Churches themselves suffered under Communism, this instant demand is one which in many areas it would be immensely difficult to meet. But the fact that the need is a real one and widely felt is itself a striking affirmation that the yearning for the 'things of the Spirit' lies deep within the human heart.

Freedom and solidarity in the West

What, then, of the West? If Communism was the abuse of solidarity and denial of freedom, then the West suffers from a distortion of freedom and a fractured solidarity.

The Czech President, Vaclav Havel, writing some years before the so-called velvet revolution, had a stark message for the West from the experience of Communism:

> I think that, with respect to the relation of Western Europe to the totalitarian systems, no error could be greater than the one looming largest: that of failure to understand the totalitarian systems for what they ultimately are—a convex mirror of all modern civilization and a harsh, perhaps final call for global recasting of that civilization's self-understanding.[2]

His view was that corresponding to the totalitarian state in the East was an 'omnipotent dictatorship of consumption, production, advertising, commerce, consumer culture' in the West. His diagnosis was that Western culture is in the grip of a materialist view of life, which sees the human being only as an object, and which views every aspect of life as a merely technical problem.

Of course the picture is an immensely complex one, and indeed varies between and within individual countries. But there is, I believe, truth in this analysis. The extraordinary technological advances of our age, particularly in transport and mass communications, have transformed the way we relate to one another. Science and technology continue to advance at an astonishing speed, probing ever more deeply into the nature of the universe, and now exploring even the biological make-up of humanity. The new technological age in fact presents opportunities to develop the unity of the human family, but there is also an increasing danger of human alienation and spiritual impoverishment, of social injustice, and the fragmentation of communities.

Western European culture has sanctified the authority of the individual. In a world that is seen by many to have no ultimate purpose or value, the self is seen as providing the only realm in which our experience can have meaning.

No authority external to the individual is acknowledged. This is freedom, but freedom cut loose from its bearings. In this perspective to be free is only to be unfettered, to have the widest range of choices from which to select. People are seen as consumers, who must also be free to decide their own lifestyles. The suggestion that there are any limitations on individual freedom is instinctively viewed with suspicion or even hostility. Of course, the experience of Communism has shown all too clearly the pernicious effects of denying liberty to men and women. But in celebrating freedom as an absolute value, Western Europeans have perhaps lost sight of the fact that the pursuit of freedom of choice is not an end in itself. What matters more is what we do with this freedom. Some choices enslave us; other choices liberate; they are life-giving when they are consonant with the truth about us. True freedom is not having many options from which to select, but rather about acting responsibly, wisely, and well. It is the truth that sets us free. And the loss of this insight has led to a distortion of freedom. Let me quote from the Final Declaration of the 1992 Synod of European Bishops:

> ... the question of the relation of freedom with truth, which modern European culture has often conceived in opposition to each other, seems very important, since in fact freedom and truth are order-ed to each other in such a way that neither can be achieved without the other. Likewise it is crucial to resolve other oppositions, connected with this one: freedom and justice, freedom and solidarity, freedom and mutual communion. For the person, whose greatest dignity is freedom, is fulfilled not by holding back, but by self giving. (4)

This leads me to reflect on Western European attitudes to solidarity, and to see how in a sense solidarity has been opposed to freedom. It is certainly true that even within the more prosperous societies of Western Europe there are many who are effectively excluded from the material benefits enjoyed by the majority. Poverty, poor housing, unemployment, lack of health care, and education are stark evidence of an absence of solidarity at home, and the growing disparity in wealth between the North and the South reveals how little global solidarity counts for in international relations. But there are contradictory signs. Solidarity in Western Europe is nonetheless present in many striking ways, for instance in the widespread concern for human rights; in the astonishing explosion of awareness of environmental issues and the interdependence of humanity and the rest of creation; in the heartfelt and genuine concern of many people in Europe for global poverty. These are all precious seeds of hope.

It would, therefore, be a mistake to say simply that solidarity in Western Europe is missing. But to live in solidarity with others is often seen as an option for some rather than an obligation upon all. The truth, of course, is otherwise. Each of us was born into a family, into a community, and into the single human family. These are not associations of individuals which we chose to join. We are irrevocably bound to them through birth. We are all members of the same family whether we like it or not. Human solidarity is no more than a recognition of our shared humanity, and our responsibility for others flows from this.

Recognizing true solidarity, therefore, helps us to see freedom in a new context and to recognize that it is a gift with a moral and spiritual purpose. But there is a lack of agreement in Europe today about the reality of such moral and spiritual claims. The reality of objective values is disputed, and many doubt that there is ultimately any transcendent purpose to life. This is perhaps one reason why freedom as a value has become so predominant, and why there is more emphasis simply on having

choices than on what human beings can become by
choosing well.

Underlying the diverging and even contradictory under-
standings of freedom and solidarity in Europe is a deeper
uncertainty about what it is to be human. Ultimately the
answer to the question 'What is humanity?' is to be
found in Christ. '. . . Only in the mystery of the Incarnate
Word,' the Vatican II Council fathers said, 'does the
mystery of man take on light. For Adam, the first man,
was a type of him who was to come (Rom. 5.14), Christ
the Lord. Christ the new Adam, in the very revelation of
the mystery of the Father and of his love, fully reveals
man to himself and brings to light his most high calling'
(*Gaudium et Spes* 22).

The Church in Europe today

It is the Church's task to provide a richer vision of
human life and destiny to satisfy the deepest needs and
longings of many people today who are restless and
searching. She does so by pointing to him who is the
way, the truth and the life. It is striking that there seems
to be a widespread thirst for authentic religious experience
on the part of many people in Europe. There is a spiritual
hunger which is often unrecognized, much less acknowledged. Some may distrust the institutional Church, but
many seek an experience that matters to them and which
is real. This yearning for a direct encounter with God is a
precious gift; it is part of God's enduring and transforming presence in the world. For the truth is that there is a
space in the human heart which only God can fill.

The Church, the sacrament or instrumental sign of
intimate union with God and of unity with the whole
human race, has been described in many ways. It is the
Body of Christ, the Bride of Christ, the Temple of the
Holy Spirit, the People of God. 'Since the Second Vatican

Council much has been done to make the Church, as communion, more clearly understood . . .', we read in the Final Report of the Extraordinary Synod of Bishops gathered in Rome in 1985. The early Christian community was characterized in the Acts of the Apostles (2.42) as being faithful 'to the teaching of the apostles, to *koinonia*, to the breaking of bread'. These were the essential sacred realities which were the life of the community, with its two focal points, the Word of God and the Eucharist. Baptism is the entry into this communion which is the Church, but also into that communion with God through Jesus Christ in the Holy Spirit. It is in this context that I draw your attention to a fine passage from the Final Declaration of the 1992 Synod of European Bishops:

> . . . the God of Christians is not a solitary God, but God living in the communion of love of Father, Son and Holy Spirit. This love was revealed most profoundly in the Son's self-emptying. Hence the communion of love and self-emptying are at the heart of the Gospel, to be preached to Europe and the whole world, so that there may be a new encounter between the Word of Life and the various cultures.
>
> This synthesis of truth, love and communion, drawn from the witness of the life and Paschal mystery of Christ, in which God is revealed to us as one and three, constitutes the meaning and foundation of our whole Christian life and morality, which, contrary to popular opinion, is not opposed to freedom—since the new law is the grace of the Holy Spirit—but is at once its condition and fruit. From these sources can be born a culture of mutual self-giving and communion, which finds its fulfilment in self-sacrifice and daily work for the common good. (4)

In the encounter between the gospel and European cultures today we have to seek God in each situation. We must learn from the insights of those who are trying earnestly to live out their Christian vocation in circumstances very different from our own. For the life of any Christian community is never divorced from its cultural roots. In language, custom, history, and geography each local church has its own story which forms part of its identity. The Council of European Bishops' Conferences (CCEE) symposium has provided us with an opportunity to broaden and deepen our sense of *communio* as that in which each local church participates through word and sacrament. In this way we are all helped to see more profoundly our religious identity, expressed through membership of the local church, in its universal context. The same Holy Spirit working within the Church and within each and every believer is the foundation of our unity and union (cf *Lumen Gentium* 13).

The Church does not exist for its own sake. The Church has a mission to the world. We come now to examine the specific tasks of the Church in Europe today in the context of our themes of freedom and solidarity. The list of five tasks I present to you is personal to me and, inevitably, selective; others would doubtless have a different list.

Prayer and witness to the gospel

The first task for the Church concerns prayer and Christian witness. The Church in every age has needed the commitment of contemplatives and the example of martyrs to inspire all her members to prayer and to witness. The contemplative orders are at the heart of the Church's life and mission, and essential to it. Their lives of loving intimacy with God remind all the baptized that union with God in faith and charity is the vocation of each of them. I recall words written by Paul VI in 1975: 'The world is calling for evangelizers to speak to it of a God whom the evangelists themselves should know and be familiar with as if they could see the invisible' (*Evangelii Nuntiandi* 76). Note those last words: 'as if they could see the invisible'. The eyes of faith enable us to see, beyond the limitation of our minds and senses, that Reality which explains all things, which is God. Ten years later Pope John Paul II speaking to the CCEE symposium in 1985 said that we need heralds of the gospel who 'are experts in humanity, who know the depths of the human heart, who can share the joys and hopes, the agonies and distress of people today, but are at the same time contemplatives who have fallen in love with God.'

Witnessing to Christ has never been easy. After all, we have been told that we must be prepared to suffer for the sake of the Gospel. The Church has a special esteem for her martyrs. The Church in Communist countries has suffered grievously. We in the West have admired those witnesses to the faith in Central and Eastern Europe. There are, I am sure, many unsung heroes and heroines who have been fine examples of Christian fidelity and fortitude. Such witnesses, in whom Christ shines forth, are crucial to the life of the Church at all times. This has been admirably expressed by Jósef Tischner reflecting on the experience of persecution in Communist Europe:

> ... there is quite simply no faith without heroism. Christianity is strong through the blood of its martyrs, for the testimony of blood is far more important than any instruction. We do not mean martyrs for abstract ideas, but martyrs for love of one's neighbour: my neighbour is an absolute value for me.[3]

Justice and peace

The Church's first and fundamental task, then, is prayer and witness to the Gospel. But the Church also has a duty to advocate justice and to cultivate peace. Paul VI in *Evangelii Nuntiandi* stressed the importance of the relationship between evangelization and questions of justice and peace. He said that,

> Between evangelization and human advancement—development and liberation—there are in fact profound links. These include . . . links of the eminently evangelical order, which is that of charity: how in fact can one proclaim the new commandment without promoting in justice and in peace the true, authentic advancement of man? (EN 31)

He then recalled his own address to the Third General Assembly of the Synod of Bishops in 1974 where he said that it is impossible to accept

> that in evangelization one could or should ignore the importance of the problems so much discussed today, concerning justice, liberation, development and peace in the world. This would be to forget the lesson which comes to us from the Gospel concerning love of our neighbour who is suffering and in need. (EN 31)

Both parts of Europe at the present time are experiencing severe economic and social difficulties. The transformation of post-Communist economies from command to market based systems has led to a massive increase in unemployment. At the same time a worldwide recession has resulted in more unemployment in the economies of Western Europe. This situation has given rise to many complex issues which are economic in part but which also have a moral aspect.

One example is the extent to which Western governments are prepared to liberalize trade with their Eastern neighbours. The European Community still imposes tight import controls on many of the products where post-Communist countries are most competitive, such as steel,

textiles and food. Should these restrictions be further
lifted? I am not competent to judge the specific economic
and financial details, but I do say that there is a moral
dimension as well. This must not be overlooked and it is
the reason for the Church's concern. A contribution to
lasting peace and stability in post-Communist Europe can
perhaps be made if Western Europe makes some short-
term sacrifices, and gives more assistance to countries
struggling to regain economic strength, leading to a wider
and more firmly based prosperity.

It is important, however, to guard against promoting
only a limited solidarity in the economic sphere. The
universal dimension of solidarity I spoke of earlier leads
us to ask what responsibility Europe has to the developing world. There is a real danger that efforts are being
so concentrated on the rebuilding of post-Communist
Europe, and on the West's own difficulties, that the grave
situation in the developing world will be forgotten.

The churches must work with others to ensure that
the new Europe does not abandon solidarity with the
Third World, and that it contributes to the just development of all peoples. Many less developed countries face
crippling external debts and severe restrictions on international trade. What is needed is not only emergency aid
from the wealthier in Europe, but the deep engagement of
all Europeans in the welfare of the world's poorest people.
It is only by demonstrating a real international solidarity
that the whole of Europe can find a way to its moral
health. If it shuts out the outside world, and attempts to
create a separate wealthy bloc, it will risk being suffocated
by materialism.

The second issue I will mention in connection with
justice is migration and the flow of refugees. The advent
of market forces and disciplines in Central and Eastern
Europe has encouraged many, particularly younger men
and women, to move from settled communities in search
of greater prosperity and job opportunities. Migration

can present a tension between freedom and solidarity of people: the freedom to move, to seek work, and the solidarity of communities affected. There are also many refugees from the former Yugoslavia and other parts of the world. Strains can be placed on communities, and there is in many countries a worrying rise of right-wing extremism and xenophobia. These pressures admit of no easy solution.

It must be recognized that communities have legitimate anxieties when faced with possible large influxes of people, and that governments have a proper duty to ensure that such matters are dealt with in an orderly way. But it is important for the churches to stress the moral imperative to help those in need. They should also emphasize the potential cultural gain from communities embracing foreigners. How much was lost to Spain, for instance, in expelling the Jewish community five hundred years ago. How much lost to Central and Eastern European States in the post-war era through the tragic losses of whole populations through the Holocaust and its aftermath. Humanity has a coat of many colours, and we should glory in the mixture.

This leads me once more to the question of peace, and the disturbing resurgence of nationalism in Europe. This is all too evident in the appalling and continuing agony of former Yugoslavia. This war, fought with unbelievable cruelty, is a grim lesson to humanity that the collapse of Communism has not crushed evil in Europe. At the end of the twentieth century, even after the experience of two world wars, the human capacity to obscure or deny the humanity of one's neighbour on ethnic grounds is not only undiminished, but even newly unleashed. Among the very many victims of the war in Bosnia, the Muslims in particular have suffered from what amounts to genocide. This action has no precedent in the post-war history of Europe, and the concerted effort to eliminate a nation, its culture and its heritage must be abhorrent to all people of good-will. It is frightening that a sovereign state, recognized by the international community, is being dismembered primarily because of the religious and ethnic background of a substantial part of the population.

The curse of nationalism, which haunts Europe's past, resulted from the elevation of national identity into a false absolute. But more important than national identity is our common humanity. What we share as human beings is far more important than what divides us. In gospel terms we can say that solidarity constantly resists being limited. It is, of course, necessary for local loyalties to be fostered: family, region, nation, European, but these solidarities do not exclude each other, and none should override the basic solidarity which we share with all humanity. The Church must witness to this. And she must constantly guard against the temptation to allow herself to be used in support of exclusive regional or national identities. We have to recognize that many communities in Europe with strong traditions of religious adherence also have the deepest social and cultural roots in the historical development of the continent. It is not easy in such circumstances to separate religious identity and cultural identity. But the principle of solidarity leads us to seek always to balance loyalty to fellow citizens with a wider loyalty to mankind. Solidarity has an inescapable universal dimension.

Europe is now multi-cultural to a degree unimaginable in previous generations. Major European cities all have substantial ethnic minorities living within them. As opportunities for communications and travel increase, European societies will become steadily less homogenous. I believe this fact offers a great opportunity to combat nationalist pressures. For, if handled positively, it could help more people to see their common identity as residing in membership of the same community rather than exclusively in a shared ethnic, religious, or social background. And this will assist European societies to promote an idea of citizenship which is not based on ethnic or social descent. The churches in Europe have a key role here in promoting peace by proclaiming the dignity of each person made in the image and likeness of God. We have to advocate an inclusive and open solidarity founded on love and respect for the stranger, and oppose an exclusive and closed solidarity founded on indifference or even fear of the stranger.

Immediately after the fall of the Communist dictatorships there was much talk of the 'peace dividend'. Of course, the Cold War was enormously expensive in armaments and much of these resources are now thankfully being put to better use. Underlying the idea of such a dividend, however, was the thought that while preventing war is expensive, peace should be free. The truth is otherwise. Promoting true peace is harder than preventing war, because it involves us in constant self-sacrifice. For peace depends on justice. Peace is not merely the absence of war, but the fashioning of communities based on tolerance, mutual respect and constant regard for the common good. Building up true solidarity is difficult and costly.

Christian unity and other faiths

These, then, are some aspects of the Church's concern for peace and justice in Europe founded on her concern for human dignity and the unity of humanity. And this leads me to the third task of the Church today, which is the need for Christian unity. The Church is the sign and source of reconciliation between God and humanity. And to fulfil her mission in society the Church must herself be a united and reconciled community. One fundamental role for the Church in Europe, therefore, is to pursue and foster Christian unity. It is for this reason that the Holy Father, in his letter to the Presidents of CCEE in January

1986, dwelt on this most significant point. I would like to quote what he said at some length:

> Europe has a special importance for the history of the Church and for the progressive expansion, beginning in apostolic times, of the gospel message throughout the world. The difficulties now being experienced by Europe must lead Christians to gather their strength, rediscover their origins and give fresh life to those genuine values which sealed the spiritual unity of the continent and fed the bright flame of a civilization from which so many other nations of the earth have drawn.
>
> The Christian civilization of Europe has its root in two venerable traditions which have developed through a centuries-long process with distinct but complementary features. These are the Latin tradition and the Eastern tradition, each one having its own theological, liturgical and ascetical peculiarities, but each filled with the inexhaustible wealth of the one revealed Truth. For there is one soul giving them inspiration, one original source and one final goal. Since in the course of the centuries there occurred the painful break between East and West, a break from which the Church still suffers today, there is a particularly urgent obligation to restore unity, so that the beauty of the Spouse of Christ may shine forth in all its radiance. For the two traditions, precisely because they are complementary, are, when taken separately, in a way imperfect. It is through a meeting and harmonization of the two that they can be reciprocally completed, and offer more adequate interpretation of the 'mystery hidden for ages and generations but now made manifest to his saints' (Col. 1.26).

Furthermore, Europe is the continent in which there occurred that other rending of the 'seamless

garment' which goes under the name of the 'Protes-
tant Reformation'. It is obvious to everyone what a
serious obstacle to the evangelizing effort in the
modern world is constituted by this situation of
division. Every individual must therefore strive with
complete commitment in the cause of ecumenism,
in order that, through the contribution of all,
progress towards unity will not only not cease but
will rather experience that speeding up which the
most fervent souls, moved by the Spirit, long for.
Europe is the original 'homeland' of these religious
divisions; to Europe therefore belongs in a particular
way the task of seeking the most suitable means for
overcoming those divisions as soon as possible. And
the better co-ordinated this search is the more effective it will be.

The search for Christian unity, therefore, remains of
paramount importance for the Church in witnessing effectively to a divided and fragmented Europe. There is a
further aspect too, which is the importance of building
up closer relationships with the Jewish, Muslim, and
other faith communities in Europe. I have already referred
to the worrying rise in xenophobia in some parts of
Europe, and there are disturbing signs of renewed anti-
Semitism. It is increasingly important for the Christian
churches to denounce such action. The responsibility of
Christian Europe in respect of anti-Semitism has to be
acknowledged, and the churches have an urgent obligation to foster closer relations with our Jewish brothers
and sisters.

Of no less importance is Islam. In the aftermath of the
Cold War some in Europe have been quick to identify
Islam as the outsider, that against which the new Europe
has to define itself. The truth is, of course, that Islam has
been an important part of European culture for several
centuries. The Tartars in Poland, the Pomaks of Bulgaria,

the Gypsy Muslims of Romania, and the Muslims of Bosnia are just a few of the Muslim communities which have long formed part of the rich mosaic of our continent. Today, there are large Muslim communities in many European countries.

Dialogue with Islam is particularly important and there is much work to be done. One area of dialogue with Islam which the Church in Europe can contribute is its experience over the last few centuries whereby Church and State in European societies have gradually separated, to the point where in most European societies now the State professes little or no explicit religious affiliation. There is an increasing recognition that it is possible for citizens of the same State whose laws allow religious freedom and promote human dignity to hold divergent religious beliefs and live together in peace with mutual respect. This process of separation has not been quick or painless, but the Church accepts that she can still be true to herself in a plural society.

Here especially is one aspect where the experience of local churches in Europe is diverse. I believe, however, that accepting the reality of a plural society in no way diminishes the Church's mission, and on the contrary can even lead to a closer realization of Jesus' words, 'My kingdom is not of this world.' Moreover, as more lay people come to play an increasingly active role in the life of the Church in European society, the presence of the Church will perhaps come to be identified less with the public institution, and more with the work and lives of the whole People of God.

The role of the laity

Indeed, giving due emphasis to the role of the laity in the Church is the fourth task I wish to highlight. The Church's understanding of *communio* is that of a body in which each of the parts works for the good of all. Each member of the Church bears responsibility in his or her own way. There is a growing awareness of the participatory role of the laity and a willingness among lay people to take responsibility in the Church. Many lay people have a strong sense of vocation and they should play an increasingly active role. The Holy Father, in *Christifideles Laici*, wrote:

> The eyes of faith behold a wonderful scene: that of a countless number of lay people, both women and men, busy at work in their daily life and activity, oftentimes far from view and quite unacclaimed by the world, unknown by the world's great personages, but nonetheless looked upon in love by the Father, untiring labourers who work in the Lord's vineyard. Confident and steadfast through the power of God's grace, these are the humble yet great builders of the Kingdom of God in history. (CL 17)

The same document also stressed the importance of the role of women in the life of the Church and the development of society, and echoed the statement made at the Second Vatican Council: 'Since in our days women are taking an increasingly active share in the whole life of society, it is very important that they participate more widely also in the various fields of the Church's apostolate' (*Apostolicam Actuositatem* 9). In an age where discrimination and abuse of women are still sadly prevalent, it is all the more important that the Church opposes such victimization. She must also emphasize that women as well as men are made sharers by baptism and confirmation of the threefold mission of Jesus Christ—priest, prophet, and king—and are thereby enabled to play a full part in the fundamental mission of evangelization, always respecting, as I would think, the differences between men and women (cf CL 51).

There should be no artificial separation made by lay people between membership of the Church and citizenship of human society. I would like to quote again from *Christifideles Laici*:

> There cannot be two parallel lives in their existence: on the one hand, the so-called 'spiritual' life, with its values and demands; and on the other, the so-called 'secular' life, that is, life in a family, at work, in social relationships, in the responsibilities of public life and in culture. The branch, engrafted to the vine which is Christ, bears its fruit in every sphere of existence and activity. In fact, every area of the lay faithful's lives, as different as they are, enters into the plan of God, who desires that these very areas be the 'places in time' where the love of Christ is revealed and realized for both the glory of the Father and service of others. Every activity, every situation, every precise responsibility—as, for example, skill and solidarity in work, love and dedication in the family and the education of children, service to society and public life and the promotion of truth in the area of culture—are the occasions ordained by Providence for a 'continuous exercise of faith, hope and charity'. (CL 59)

It is one of the errors of our age to have established false dichotomies between religion and life, and between sacred and secular. The real distinction is not between religion and life, but between what is real and what is illusory: between a life lived in the truth, and a life based on false hopes. Our faith reveals the truth about God and the truth about humanity, and so it is that St Irenaeus could say: 'The Glory of God is the human person fully alive.'

There is no 'secular' realm from which God is absent. His presence in the world may be hidden and even denied, but God is everywhere. Therefore we must seek

God in all the experiences of life and in all that is. It is the particular role of the laity to sanctify the temporal and to work towards transforming that temporal order so that the presence of God within it may be recognized and acknowledged. The truth is that the Church, as *communio*, has not a purely spiritual character but is intimately involved in the building of the Kingdom in the human city. The new heaven and the new earth are not only to be longed for in the next life, but are to be established here and now. And in this task all the members of the body of Christ, lay women and men, religious women and men, priests and bishops, have important roles to play.

The family

I come now to the fifth task for the Church in Europe today. It is the support of the family. The Christian family, described by the Second Vatican Council as *ecclesia domestica*, has a key role in building up the Kingdom of God in history. In Europe today the pressures on families are often intense, and the Church clearly must strengthen the integrity of family life.

It is striking that in the *European Values Study 1981– 1990* the family is the one institution which is everywhere seen as overwhelmingly important.[4] Yet the high value attached to family life is accompanied by a growing reluctance to tolerate unsatisfactory marital relationships, and attitudes to divorce in many countries have steadily become more liberal in recent years.

The family is the basis of any human society. In a healthy family children learn freedom and solidarity. They are able to love, because they have first been loved by their parents. A healthy family naturally brings out the connections between the virtues, and inculcates values which allow for a richer life. It is little wonder that in societies that have lost a sense of shared values, and that elevate self-fulfilment above self-sacrifice, family life should have been subjected to such strain and stress. In fact one principal reason for the breakdown in family life is surely a perceived opposition between freedom and commitment. The ideal of freedom as choice, which I spoke of earlier, has undermined the ideal of freedom as self-giving, which has to be at the heart of married love. The inner dynamic of family commitment calls forth solidarity. As the Holy Father wrote in *Familiaris Consortio*:

> The relationships between the members of the family community are inspired and guided by the law of 'free giving'. By respecting and fostering personal dignity in each and every one as the only basis for value, this free giving takes the form of heartfelt acceptance, encounter and dialogue, disinterested availability, generous service and deep solidarity. (FC 43)

The future of European societies rests as much on the health of the family as on anything else. The importance many people in Europe attach to the family is a positive sign, and the Church clearly has an urgent duty to do all she can to help in realizing this ideal.

Prayer and witness, advocating justice and peace, Christian unity and relations with other faiths, the role of the laity, and finally the family—these are my list of tasks for the Church in Europe today. We have to approach them all in humility, conscious of our own weakness, and yet in confidence, aware of the intimate and eternal love of God for humanity and all creation. The Church exists to unite and to reconcile. She promotes a universal solidarity founded on love, and speaks to the world of a vision of transcendence, of the unity of all things in Christ.

Notes

1. Jósef Tischner, 'Christianity in the Post-Communist Vacuum', *The Keston Journal*, vol. 20, nos 3 and 4.
2. Vaclav Havel, *Living in Truth*, Faber and Faber, 1987, p. 145; quoted by Alan M. Suggate, 'Personal Responsibility: Hayek and Havel in Christian Perspective', *The Keston Journal*, vol. 20, nos 3 and 4, 1992.
3. Tischner, *The Keston Journal*.
4. *European Values Study 1981–90 Summary Report*, eds. David Barker, Lock Halman and Astrid Vloet, published by the Gordon Cook Foundation on behalf of the European Values Group, chapter 9.

FOUR

The desire for God

It would not be unduly dramatic to claim that Western Europe, at least, is suffering from a spiritual and moral crisis of immense proportions. It could be argued, too, that we stand before one of those periods in history which will determine the future for centuries. It is perhaps to be ranked with the fall of the Roman Empire, the emergence of the Middle Ages, the flowering of the Renaissance, the Age of Enlightenment, and the onset of the Industrial Revolution. As in all those periods of profound change, our present age offers both danger and opportunity: the threat of disaster and the promise of growth.

Europe's spiritual fragments

It is often remarked that developed, industrialized countries in this century are witnessing an unprecedented decline in religious practice, together with an indifference, if not a hostility, towards the institutional Church and a revolution in moral values and behaviour. Some will argue that the erosion of belief in God as Father and Creator, in the divinity of Christ, in the concept of redemption, and in life after death will lead gradually but inevitably to a changed perception of human dignity and the sanctity of human life. The threat is obvious enough. The dangers are real.

Jacques Maritain, in his book *True Humanism*, pointed out that from the dawn of modern times thinkers like Descartes, Rousseau and Kant fashioned an image of 'man', defiantly independent, splendidly rational, basically good. Man's universe was complete and closed. There was no need for God, for divine revelation, for grace. There was no place for a Sovereign Good to solicit his will. Man was the summit and the measure of the universe.

It did not take long, says Maritain, for such self-confidence to disintegrate. The rationalist concept of human personality was dealt a severe blow by the emergence last century of a new orthodoxy from the world of biology. We may now be engaged in a reappraisal of the theory of evolution, but Charles Darwin's hypotheses at that time caused confusion to Christian and rationalist alike. What happens to mankind's pretensions if man is no more than 'the naked ape'?

Even more destructive were the theories of Freud. Christians have always seen, as Pascal did, that the human heart is hollow and full of evil, but they have also recognized human greatness and spiritual dignity. But those who had embraced rationalism and materialism were left, after Freud, with a fallen idol. The purely natural being, the heroic, quasi-divine figure lay in ruins. The human personality, its conscious dignity, was seen as a deception, masking turbulent depths of instinct and desire.

Our own experience shows us how in this century

human dignity has suffered further attacks both existentially and philosophically. It has been a period of almost endless pain, written largely in human blood. Inevitably, respect for life has been eroded. The innocent civilian, the casual bystander is taken as a legitimate target by state and terrorist alike.

Less dramatic, but also important, have been the social changes brought about by the rapid, almost universal spread of urbanization and industrialization. We are promised, or threatened, a future shaped by advanced technology, automation and the microchip. All this is likely to have major repercussions on our work-patterns, our social lives, our families. It may well affect our sense of community, our way of interreacting with others. It will dwarf the effects of the Industrial Revolution.

Human dignity, human individuality, have also come under heavy pressure this century from new and destructive ideologies. Nazism, Fascism, and Communism have been the major secular heresies of our age. In their system, as in racialist regimes, the individual has no absolute, inviolable value. On occasions he or she can be sacrificed for a greater good. Some indeed can be safely disregarded as non-persons. The threat from Western materialism and consumerism seems much less destructive at first sight. There is no apparatus of repression. There are no signs of physical ill-treatment. Living standards are often extremely high. Yet Western capitalism can be exploitative and unfeeling. Many in the Third World criticize bitterly the activities of multi-national corporations. Workers in the Western democracies seem to be valued for what they produce rather than for what they are. At times of economic difficulties, they are the first victims of recession and are relegated to the dole queues with routine expressions of regret.

In the writings of the Existentialists we find expressed a bleak loneliness, a sense that life is absurd and pointless. We are puzzled and perhaps wryly amused, but always alone. Each of us—in the existentialist view—creates our own identity, but we are creators without the guidance and help of any other hand. Deprived of any sense of who God is and what we are, there can be no healing, no direction, no meaning. It is an attitude that was shaped by the tragedies and despair of this century. The devastation of two world wars, the social tensions created by industrialization and unemployment, the abyss of human cruelty revealed in the horrors of the Holocaust and the Stalinist terror brought Europe to its knees, exhausted emotionally and psychologically, and left Europeans war-weary, disillusioned, and unsure of their humanity.

In such a society it is little wonder that there should be so much personal aimlessness, apathy, and frustration. If we frequently have lost the assurance that there are genuine values and a natural ordering of desires, we easily fall victim to the pressure of the present. If we have no reliable compass to steer by, we convince ourselves that the only course is to be true to our changing self. It is not surprising that commitment and consistency suffer. We are buffeted fiercely by our emotions and pulled this way and that by conflicting desires. The centre cannot hold; there is fragmentation of the human spirit; it affects us all to a greater or lesser extent; it is the prevailing mood of the moment.

In the past, personal insecurity and lack of coherence could be masked by a more unquestioning acceptance of authority and reliance on authority figures. Today there is profound and widespread scepticism, bred of war experience, political, social and economic corruption, and the growing influence of mass media, which maintain little or no respect for establishment figures or the erstwhile pillars of society. It has caused individuals to believe that they are on their own, without heroes, without role models. It has led in literature and drama to the emergence of the anti-hero. It affects social attitudes, coinciding with the growth of popular democracy and the overthrow of in-

herited privilege. It has had its effect on religious struc-
tures and the stability of church communities. There is a
crisis of credibility, and religious authority now has to be
gained and not presumed. Equally clearly there is a
tendency among Europeans and North Americans in particular to be eclectic, to pick and choose their own
mixture of beliefs and to be suspicious of any claim to
authority. It helps to explain also the modern preoccupation with religious experience and the comparative neglect
of revelation. Here, at least, it is felt that direct experience
provides a reliable guide.

We pursue our search for wholeness in an often fragmented and broken world. Division and fragmentation
are to be found both in the inner world of our personal
consciousness and in the society we have fashioned for
ourselves. They exist alongside evidence of enduring goodness and undoubted growth.

A vivid gospel episode provides an insight into our
inner disunity. In the country of the Gadarenes, Christ
encountered a man with an unclean spirit. He challenged
the devil: 'What is your name?' 'My name is legion', he
answered, 'for there are many of us' (Mark 5.9). The
destructiveness is dramatically described: 'The man lived
in the tombs and no one could secure him any more, even
with a chain . . . All night and all day, among the tombs
and in the mountains, he would howl and gash himself
with stones' (Mark 5.3–7). Driven out of the man, the
legion of devils swept a herd of pigs to its destruction.
The man, restored to his senses and now fully clothed,
sat at the feet of Jesus and begged to be allowed to
follow him wherever he went. Instead he was sent home
to tell his people what the mercy of God had achieved
and how wholeness had been restored.

Here we are in the presence of profound truth. It is an
ancient wisdom that when the first human beings refused
to obey God they upset the order in themselves and
consequently in society. The disobedience of Adam and

Eve was followed by murderous rivalry between Cain and Abel. Anarchy entered the world. The divine capacity in us to know and to choose was enslaved to self, to personal and selfish objectives. Disregard for God and neighbour led individuals along the ways of death. The passionate pursuit of personal fulfilment at any cost did not result in greater satisfaction and happiness. Instead we all became liable to an inner disintegration and to self-destruction. Despite the redemption and the restoration of all things in Christ our wayward selves still suffer from the tug of passion, the stirrings of pride, and the frequent blindness of selfishness.

The turning point

We see that the human genius has built up in our age an imposing scientific and technological empire, but that our sinfulness has made us slaves in our own kingdom. Not harmony but conflict reigns between individuals and between nations. These fundamental divisions are the product of sin, for sin is separation: we are separated from God, and from each other.

When an individual realizes his or her personal sinfulness, it ought not to lead to depression or to a sense of hopelessness; instead it should lead to an act of humility before God. It is this which prompts the individual to seek from God what he cannot achieve for himself, namely that peace which comes from forgiveness and that oneness with God which is the foundation of true happiness. *Cor contritum et humiliatum Deus non despicies* ('A broken and contrite heart, O God, you will not despise' Ps. 50) is the prayer of a person who is beginning to experience that change of heart, of which the gospel speaks. It is a prayer full of hope, a starting-point for nations as well as for individuals. It is the first step in that search for God which is the ultimate purpose and joy of all living. In a confused and not always conscious way, every individual is called by God to embark on that search. Yet at every stage the contradictions and the consequences of sin persist.

It is the heart of the individual that is divided and needs to be healed and made whole. The primacy of the rule of God in the heart of each person is the foundation upon which justice and peace will be built. There must first be repentance, for there is sin in the world and we are all sinners. Once there is repentance, reconciliation will follow. And so the words of the Lord, 'the kingdom of God is at hand; repent and believe the Gospel' (Mark 1.15), speak to us today as urgently as they spoke to past ages. They are words which not only contain an admonition but also provide the essential starting-point for the process of healing ourselves and society and so of achieving unity and peace.

Indeed, there is evidence of such a change. Although violence is rife in our time, there is paradoxically a more widespread struggle for human rights, and among many people there is a greater sensitivity to the dignity of the individual. Not only is torture widely condemned and outlawed, but the abolition of the death penalty, the renunciation of corporal punishment and the movement against blood sports and vivisection are evidence that violence against other humans and the animal kingdom is seen to be degrading and loathsome. Coupled with this is the much heightened sense of human dignity and equality. Many countries have already seen a quite remarkable revolution in the acceptance of women's rights and equality. Discrimination against minorities and those hitherto regarded as inferior is further proof of a more humane and respectful attitude towards others who differ from us. Disregard for the right to life of unborn children contrasts strangely with greater concern for the development and welfare of the child and the handicapped adult. Indifference to the authority, doctrine, and worship of the churches co-exists with some evidence of greater moral seriousness, of a more mature acceptance of individual responsibility and often with an eager search for the riches of the spirit, for prayer and for the things of God. Sometimes it seems that affluence and achievement reveal to modern man and woman, in a striking way, their spiritual emptiness and their hunger for the transcendent. That emptiness must be filled, that hunger satisfied.

It is, in my view, clear from the history of the human race and from the literature of every culture that men and women do experience a persistent and insatiable hunger. They are driven by that hunger always to seek new experience. But they suffer endless frustration since they cannot grasp the deeper significance of their hunger nor how it can be satisfied. Their hunger expresses itself in two ways, which most people will recognize from their own experience. Every individual searches for meaning in life, an explanation for their own existence and for their own experiences. At the same time, every individual searches for happiness, for that ecstasy which is found in its most intense form in the experience of love. The search for meaning and for happiness is, in point of fact, a single search. It seeks what lies above, beyond, and outside the self. It reaches out to grasp this reality, this transcendence, this Absolute. And—here is the deepest level of truth—this reality and transcendence is found to be a living God, a personal and infinite God.

I believe we all experience this search and this hunger to a greater or lesser extent. But I also believe firmly that this is our human way of describing and experiencing an even more intense search and hunger, that of God for us. It really is like a cosmic game of hide and seek. We have all of us, as adults, played hide and seek with children. With a child's utter seriousness they believe they are seeking some hidden person while, all the time, we ensure that we will always be found. If the child takes too long, or seems to be lost, we go looking for the child. Our search for God, basic to our human nature, brings us sooner or later to that encounter with God which he had always intended. In that encounter I believe we can truly find ourselves, our meaning and our happiness.

The personal fragmentation to which I have referred is part, but not the entire picture. As I already indicated, alongside fragmentation are found many indications of new life and the presence of God's Spirit in our inmost selves. Original sin still plays its part but the image of God even in the worst of us is never entirely effaced. Mother Julian of Norwich in one of her best-known revelations describes how she saw all reality as a hazelnut in the palm of her hand. She writes:

> I marvelled that it could last for I thought it might have crumbled to nothing, it was so small. And the answer came to my mind, 'It lasts and ever shall because God loves it.' And all things have being through the love of God. In this little thing I saw three things. The first is that God made it. The second is that God loves it. The third is that God looks after it.[1]

If all things are so created, loved and protected, how much more jealously will God regard, cherish and pursue the person he has made in his own image and likeness and whom he loves eternally in Christ.

The Christian Church is not the product of human wisdom. It is not primarily motivated by humanitarian concern. It is the guardian and herald of a revelation from God and so it deals in mysteries. Mysteries are profound truths beyond the grasp of our unaided intellects, yet yielding their riches to the humble and the prayerful. The progressive revelation of God to his people in the Hebrew Scriptures and the teaching of Jesus Christ together form the substance of Christian wisdom and the inspiration for Christian living. Jesus thanked his Father for hiding these things from the learned and the clever, but revealing them to little children.

The book of Genesis, sacred to the Jewish and Christian tradition, expresses a fundamental insight into human nature:

> God said, 'Let us make man in our own image, in the image of ourselves, and let them be masters of the fish of the sea, the birds of heaven, the cattle, all the wild beasts and the reptiles that crawl upon the earth.' God created man in the image of himself, in the image of God he created him, male and female, he created them. (Gen. 1.26–7)

It is a familiar account; it contains a wealth of meaning. God, for the Jew and the Christian, is no impersonal force. He is the Creator acting with intelligence and love. From the beginning, human beings are pictured as altogether special, set apart from the rest of creation as if claiming kinship with God rather than the animal world. 'Made in the image of God'—not because they are flesh and blood but because they have within themselves a divine spark, the power of reasoning, the capacity to choose and to love. Each individual, then, reflects something of God and was destined by God to be a familiar friend, walking together with him among the delights of Paradise. Pride, self-will, disobedience, shattered the innocence of the Garden of Eden. Adam and Eve and their children, made by God and for God, rebelled against God and entered a world of conflict and sin. At war within themselves, in conflict with their neighbours, they defied God and plunged the world into darkness. The whole of the Bible tells the story of how God went in search of his human creation, of how the Good Shepherd restored the scattered flock to the sheepfold, of how the Creator refashioned that image of himself, for so long disfigured, for so long broken into fragments by sin. He remade man

and woman in the person of Jesus Christ, offering to
them a new life, a more glorious destiny.

In Jesus Christ, then, the believer perceives a twofold
reality. The eyes of faith gaze on him and see what man
and woman can be and are meant by God to be. At the
same time, the believer can trace in the features of Jesus
the image of God the Father.

> Philip said: 'Lord, let us see the Father and we shall
> be satisfied.' 'Have I been with you all this time,
> Philip?' said Jesus to him, 'and you still do not
> know me? To have seen me is to have seen the
> Father, so how can you say "Let us see the Father"?
> Do you not believe that I am in the Father and the
> Father is in me?' (John 14.8–10)

This surely is where Christianity stands alone. Central
to our faith is the belief that God became a human being.
In Jesus Christ we stand at the point of intersection
between the divine and the human; in Christ we see what
God offers to humanity and what humanity can grasp of
the divine. For two thousand years we have pondered the
significance of the incarnation. I am certain that it still
has power to transform our understanding of human
nature, although historically we have constantly failed to
live out its consequences.

In analysing the contemporary scene I have spoken
much of fragmentation, but also of new life. This implies
hope not despair. We witness in dramatic form the continuing creative act of God in our world. I turn to that
image of God as the potter in Jeremiah's prophecy: 'So I
went down to the potter's house and there he was working at his wheel. And the vessel he was making of clay
was spoiled in the potter's hand, and he reworked it into
another vessel, as it seemed good to the potter to do' (Jer.
18.1–4). As Isaiah also saw: 'Yes, O Lord, thou art our
Father; we are the clay, and thou art the potter; we are
all the work of thy hand' (Isa. 64.8). The fragmentation

we experience is not final disintegration but a stage, painful but necessary, in the reshaping of ourselves and society and the gradual emergence of a new shape and beauty. The very fact that we recognize much in ourselves and society as fragmented and imperfect implies that we are judging present reality in the light of an understanding we already have of a better and more perfect reality which we have—however dimly—already perceived. The mind of the potter is reflected—partially and imperfectly—in our human minds. As he takes the flawed vessel to recreate something new, we share the excitement of creating with him something which more nearly resembles the beauty and the order that is his. With him and under the inspiration of his Spirit it is for us to search for a greater coherence and wholeness in ourselves and in society and in our understanding of reality. Precisely because God has gifted us with this created sharing in his understanding and love we are uneasy and restless in the presence of disorder, disunity, and death. Humanity will never rest content until in Christ are shaped 'a new heaven and a new earth . . . where God will dwell with us and we shall be his people' (Rev. 21.1–3). The key to all growth and progress and to all understanding is the Word 'in whom all things are made'.

The Christian cosmos

The advent of the Third Millennium, the passing into history of the Age of Enlightenment, the evidence of a new longing for unity religiously, politically and socially, the ongoing discovery of new knowledge and new technology, all constitute new signs of the times and the coming upon us of a *kairos*, a moment of profound grace. We are being led into a more profound understanding of the Church as *koinonia*, of humanity as a single family and of our responsibility to the planet and to the cosmos.

Scientists, space-explorers and theologians alike are offering us new horizons. Unlike the bitter confrontation and polarization of science and religion in the last century, there is today a sense of convergence, of enrichment. That was brought home to me by a remarkable book of photographs taken of our planet, the moon, and the galaxy by satellites and space-shuttles, entitled *The Home Planet*. Alongside the magnificent photographs were the words of astronauts. James Irwin from America is quoted as saying:

> The Earth reminded us of a Christmas tree ornament hanging in the blackness of space. As we got further and further away it diminished in size. Finally it shrank to the size of a marble, the most beautiful marble you can imagine. The beautiful, warm, living object looked so fragile, so delicate, that if you touched it with a finger it would crumble and fall apart. Seeing this has to change a man, has to make a man appreciate the creation of God and the love of God.[2]

The believer has a distinctive contribution to make here to a newly emerging attitude to the world and to the cosmos. So much of this new knowledge has been gained since the time of the Second Vatican Council. It is for us to detect meaning, to point to the pattern and purpose inherent in created things, and to prepare for the future.

Here I must acknowledge my indebtedness to the Extraordinary Synod of Bishops gathered in Rome in 1985, which created in me an understanding of how the four constitutions of the Council might together provide a vision of the whole of reality. *Lumen Gentium* explored the inner reality of the Church as mystery and communion, needing to be nourished and shaped by the Word of God (*Dei Verbum*), and by sacrament and the offering of thanksgiving, praise, and intercession (*Sacrosanctum Concilium*), in order to fulfil its mission of reconciling, healing

and renewing the face of the earth (*Gaudium et Spes*).
That mission is expressed in the sublime words of St
Paul:

> Therefore, if anyone is in Christ, he is a new crea-
> tion; the old has passed away, behold the new has
> come. All this is from God, who through Christ
> reconciled us to himself and gave us the message of
> reconciliation; that is, in Christ God was reconciling
> the world to himself, not counting their trespass
> against them and entrusting to us the message of
> reconciliation . . . For our sake he made him to be
> sin who knew no sin so that in him we might
> become the righteousness of God. (2 Cor. 5.17–21)

In this single vision is summed up the mystery of the
Church, its place in God's universe, its glorious and
eternal destiny. Let us explore this more deeply, especially
since we are preparing to celebrate the two thousandth
anniversary of the birth of Jesus Christ, true God and
true man. The incarnation holds inexhaustible significance for us; we are now, I believe, in a position to take
the thinking and teaching of the Second Vatican Council
one stage further. It is becoming clearer that the Council
was in the most profound way a preparation for the
Third Millennium and the rediscovery of the mystery of
Christ by a world that imagined it had entered its post-
Christian phase. The mystery of Christ has to be ap-
proached by means of a deeper understanding of the
Church and of creation. Both Church and creation have
to be seen, in some analogous way, as sacraments, signs,
and effective instruments of God's presence and life, and
in both we find Christ.

Radical consequences flow from the mutual recognition
of each others' baptism by the Christian churches and
ecclesial communities. Once it was recognized that Christians truly shared the life and love of God in Christ and
had become other Christs, an irresistible dynamic towards

full communion and organic unity had been unleashed. Imperfect communion can never satisfy. Christ himself urges us forward to become one in him. He is the head of his body, the Church; he the vine, we the branches. The unity of the baptized, in Christ, has eventually to be realized in a communion of life and love which is to embrace all humanity.

But the mystery of the Church is essentially linked to the inmost reality of creation. Human disobedience and fragmentation can never obliterate or ultimately frustrate the living power and love of God that has created and sustains all things in being. All material things, all human lives, are a created reflection of the Word of God, the Second Person of the Trinity, 'in whom all things are made'. In that sense, creation can be regarded as the primary sacrament and as leading us into knowledge and love of the Creator. Here again, Christ, the Word, is the key to the meaning of existence, and again has to be seen as inevitably and ceaselessly unfolding in creation endless opportunities of life and love. It is in Christ, the Word of God, that the Church and all creation find their unity, their meaning, and their purpose. The fulfilment of all things will be when the Church which is Christ becomes the conscious unity and shared life of all humanity and when humanity offers all created things back to God in a single act of praise, thanksgiving and love. Thus *Lumen Gentium* and *Gaudium et Spes* are seen to form an integrated whole.

The new evangelization

It is in the sweep of this vision that we can begin to discern the priorities for the Church in the next millennium and the scope and scale of its evangelization. It is not for us simply to denounce the passing world and its vanities, or to foster the mistaken view that there is a dichotomy in creation, an unbridgeable chasm between the spiritual and the material, between religion and life. One God made one world, peopled by one family, in one created cosmos. Human minds are meant to explore that reality and to grasp its unity and to relate it back to its Creator. We must see all knowledge, all discovery, every advance in understanding as more profound exploration of the mind of God. We have to support the movements and the initiatives that foster international peace and justice, national, regional and global unity, and at the same time to celebrate human uniqueness, individuality, and diversity. We cannot simply wait for the Kingdom to happen, we have to pray for it ceaselessly and work for it tirelessly and recognize its every manifestation in the affairs of humanity.

In conclusion and summary I would point again to revelation, reflection, and experience, which all witness to the unity underlying all diversity. Human beings endowed with intelligence and free will in the image and likeness of their Creator are ceaselessly impelled to seek and celebrate that wholeness, that unity. It is part of the process whereby creation is enabled consciously to return to its Creator. We proclaim the good news that God insistently and continuously calls back his creation to himself through the incarnation and redemptive action of Christ. The whole process of creation is at one and the same time a going forth from unity into diversity and a returning from diversity into unity. Our search then for unity and wholeness is nothing other than a search for God, his life and love. It is our profoundest conviction that we find him in the Christ of Church and cosmos, the Lord Jesus Christ, true God and true man.

St Thomas Aquinas tells us that everyone and everything is in search of God. In this he provides the basis for all I have been saying:

All things desire God as their goal when they desire

any good whatsoever, whether by intelligent choice or the appetite of the senses or by a natural tendency which is unconscious, for nothing is good and desirable except in so far as it shares in a likeness to God.[3]

Notes

1. Julian of Norwich, *Showings*, long text, 5th chapter.
2. Kevin W. Kelly, *The Home Planet*, Queen Anne Press, 1988.
3. *Summa Theologiae* Ia, Q 44, a.4 ad 3.

The evangelization of Europe

After the Synod of 1974, Pope Paul VI reminded us:

> It is a task and mission which the vast and profound changes of present-day society make all the more urgent. Evangelizing is, in fact, the grace and vocation proper to the Church, her deepest identity. She exists in order to evangelize. (EN 14)

From the beginning we must be clear about what evangelization is. Again we turn to Pope Paul VI and his reflection on the Synod of 1974. He says:

> Evangelization will also always contain—as the foundation, centre and at the same time summit of its dynamism—a clear proclamation that, in Jesus Christ, the Son of God made man, who died and rose from the dead, salvation is offered to all, as a gift of God's grace and mercy. And not an immanent salvation, meeting material or even spiritual needs, restricted to the framework of temporal existence

and completely identified with temporal desires, hopes, affairs and struggles, but a salvation which exceeds all these limits in order to reach transcendent and eschatological salvation, which indeed has its beginning in this life but which is fulfilled in eternity. (EN 27)

Elsewhere in the same document Pope Paul enriches this concept by adding:

The Church evangelizes when she seeks to convert, solely through the divine power of the Message she proclaims, both the personal and collective consciences of people, activities in which they engage and the lives and concrete milieux which are theirs. (EN 18)

The message of salvation is universal: it penetrates and transcends human existence; it is to be proclaimed to the whole of humanity, to every level of society.

The mission field of Europe

The situation which confronts the Christian Church in our continent is complex and difficult. There are political divisions between East and West. There are profound social and cultural differences between North and South of the continent. There remain, in Europe, religious divisions caused by an often bitter religious history which has separated Catholics and Orthodox and then Catholics and Protestants. Despite these difficulties, the continent retains a spiritual unity which arises from a shared history and from common Christian values. Evangelization has to take this European reality into account. Europe is a whole but it is made up of a mosaic of peoples. The Church has to speak in the languages and in ways appropriate to the cultures of ancient and independent nations, while at the same time remaining aware of a deeper unity, a common heritage and common problems. And so the local churches and the national conferences of bishops have the obvious responsibility of bringing the gospel of Jesus Christ to their own peoples. But bishops and national conferences have the right to expect collegial support, encouragement, and help from other nations to cope with problems which transcend frontiers and affect the whole continent.

If we proclaim the Good News in Europe today, we must be aware of the different categories of people who should hear our voice: those who practise non-Christian religions, those who are atheists or humanists, those who are de-Christianized, those who have lapsed, and the general body of believers.

It may seem strange to some that at this moment in our history there should be any need for a first proclamation of Jesus Christ. In many countries of Western Europe, however, there are now large immigrant communities. Some are migrant workers; some are settling down as citizens and are making homes among us for themselves and their children. Many of these guest workers, or new immigrants, practise non-Christian religions. In Britain, for example, there are now more Muslims than Methodists. It is a post-war phenomenon which, as evangelizers, we must consider carefully.

Atheism and humanism are well-known enemies of the Gospel. They pose a different threat in the East and the West. In the West, they seep insidiously into society; they threaten to undermine its foundations. The mass media provide their proponents with access to every home. An atmosphere of secularism is gradually but effectively created. It then becomes difficult to counter, as we must, this spirit of the age. How are we to preach to those who by baptism are Christians but who by knowledge of their religion and style of life most decidedly are not? And how do we approach the well-educated who have rejected Christianity as irrelevant to their lives?

The evangelizer has an obvious responsibility to proclaim the gospel to non-Christians, to those who are de-
Christianized and to those under the sway of atheism and
militant humanism. In a different but real way he must
speak to lapsed Christians and to believers as well.

The lapsed, the non-practising, present us with a complex task. There are many degrees and kinds of lapsation.
I quote Pope Paul VI again:

> The phenomenon of the non-practising is a very
> ancient one in the history of Christianity; it is the
> result of a natural weakness, a profound inconsist-
> ency which we, unfortunately, bear deep within us.
> Today, however, it shows certain new characteris-
> tics. It is often the result of the uprooting typical of
> our time. It also springs from the fact that Christians
> live in close proximity with non-believers and conse-
> quently experience the effects of unbelief. Further-
> more, the non-practising Christians of today, more
> so than those of previous periods, seem to explain
> and justify their position in the name of an interior
> religion, of personal independence or authenticity.
> (EN 56)

The number of non-practising Christians grows alarm-
ingly. Part of the problem is that many of our Catholics
have received the sacraments, however infrequently, but
have never been brought to the point of making a personal
commitment to Christ. As we sometimes express it in
English, too many people have been 'sacramentalized' but
not 'evangelized'. We cannot ignore the problem they
present.

Nor can we neglect the task of deepening and support-
ing the faith of all believers. We cannot take for granted
their faithfulness and perseverance in such adverse situations. What is needed is not evangelization in the strict
sense of a first proclamation of the Gospel, but a more
vigorous catechesis so radical and so sustained that it

might be called a continuing evangelization. We must constantly challenge the faithful—including ourselves— with the person and message of Jesus Christ, with the fulness of the Word of God. Faith has to be deepened, strengthened, made more mature. As the Synod of 1977 recognized, this means that we must create programmes of catechesis for adults. This is 'the principal form of catechesis because it is addressed to persons who have the greatest responsibilities and the capacity to live the Christian message in its fully developed form' (*Catechesi Tradendae* 43).

Scandals

A major obstacle to the effective preaching of the gospel of Jesus Christ is the scandal of disunity among his followers. Pope Paul VI asked whether this was not one of the great sicknesses of evangelization today (EN 77). Throughout this century, in particular, Christians have experienced increasing frustration and impatience with divisions amongst themselves. Non-believers, too, can easily take refuge in criticism of Christian disharmony. It is essential that we should urgently pursue the goal of Christian unity. During his visit to Britain, Pope John Paul II signed a Common Declaration with Dr Runcie, the Anglican Archbishop of Canterbury. It contained these remarkable words:

> Our aim is not limited to the union of our two Communions alone, to the exclusion of other Christians, but rather extends to the fulfilment of God's will for the visible unity of all his people. Both in our present dialogue and in those engaged in by other Christians among themselves and with us, we recognize in the agreements we are able to reach, as well as in the difficulties which we encounter, a

renewed challenge to abandon ourselves completely
to the truth of the Gospel.

It is only by abandoning ourselves completely to the
truth of the Gospel that all our Christian divisions can be
overcome and the way to Christian unity can be pursued
humbly and yet with utter confidence. Our divisions
must not hinder any longer the urgent need for Christians
to preach together the gospel of Jesus Christ.

Disunity is not only to be found within the different
Christian bodies in Europe. In the Catholic Church itself
there exists a disunity and a polarization which is harmful
and which hinders evangelization. There exists fear and
dislike of ecumenism; the renewal of the liturgy gives rise
to profound differences of opinion; there is misunderstand-
ing and controversy over the content and methods of
catechesis; there is not agreement concerning the nature
of the Church. It is the role of bishops to be a firm
defence against disunity, to be promoters of true community in faith. There can be no unity in the diocese except
around the bishop.

Perhaps I exaggerate the harmful character of the disunity which undoubtedly exists, but I fear that internal
dissension drains away that joy and unity of purpose that
should characterize the People of God. I tend to think
that much of a bishop's time and energy can be devoted
to matters of controversy within the Church. This intro-
spection is particularly misdirected at a time when millions of people outside the Church are groping in the
dark to find a sure light for their lives. In a memorable
passage in *Evangelii Nuntiandi*, Pope Paul VI reminded
us that the world is searching for God 'in unexpected
ways' and is 'painfully experiencing the need of him'. As
bishops, and by virtue of our ordination, we have to fulfil
the role of unifying the faithful in our local church. Yet
we must then reach out to fulfil our role as evangelists.
Here—together with our people—we have to be genuinely

holy and leaders of a holy people. As Pope Paul went on
to say:

> The world is calling for evangelizers to speak to it
> of a God whom the evangelists themselves should
> know and be familiar with as if they could see the
> invisible. The world calls for and expects from us
> simplicity of life, the spirit of prayer, charity to-
> wards all, especially towards the lowly and the
> poor, obedience and humility, detachment and self-
> sacrifice. Without this mark of holiness, our word
> will have difficulty in touching the hearts of modern
> men and women. It risks being vain and sterile.
> (EN 76)

There are further obstacles to evangelization which
are partly our responsibility but are largely the fault of
society in general. The first of these—and one of the
most intractable—is the problem of war and peace.
War, indiscriminate destruction, the deliberate resort to
violence in pursuit of political aims: all these constitute
formidable barriers to the preaching and the reception
of Christ's gospel. The Church preaches the gospel of
love and reconciliation and universal brotherhood in a
sinful world where men and nations use aggression and
violence to secure their purposes. We live and work
within societies which are intent on pursuing their own
interests. How, in these circumstances, should we
preach the gospel, and how do we respond to those
politicians, military personnel, and ordinary citizens
who look to us for moral guidance?

The gospel has also to be preached today in a world
which still suffers enormously from hunger and depriva-
tion. In many ways, our continent is privileged. In some
parts of Europe we are often accused of belonging to
the 'rich man's club' and of indifference to the Third
World. We have to preach in many countries to those

who are well-fed and prosperous. How do we ensure that their eyes are opened and their hearts touched by the plight of their brothers and sisters at home as well as abroad? How do we proclaim the social teaching of the Church without losing sight of the transcendent? Christians who remain self-centred are a powerful argument against the Gospel.

This brings me to the last obstacle I shall mention. Secularism and consumerism have entered deep into the soul of many peoples in Europe. They have a profound influence on attitudes and public policies. If we are to evangelize effectively we must learn how to cultivate rich and fruitful soil. The parable of the sower speaks to us today: 'the one who received the seed in thorns is the man who hears the word, but the worries of this world and lure of riches choke the word and so he produces nothing' (Matt. 13.22). Echoing in our ears are the words of Isaiah which Jesus quoted to his apostles: 'for the heart of this nation has grown coarse, the ears are dull of hearing, and they have shut their eyes, for fear they should see with their eyes, hear with their ears, understand with their hearts and be converted and be healed by me' (Isa. 6.9–10). Power and possessions constitute a twin temptation for human beings. People are enslaved by them or persuaded to devote their lives to acquiring them. We have to demonstrate to our modern world that the pursuit of power and possessions is a snare and a delusion. The gospel must set men and women free.

These, then, are the peoples we must evangelize; these, then, are the enemies we must confront. But with what do we confront them? I put before you, as inspiration and challenge, some further words of Pope Paul VI:

> Consequently evangelization cannot but include the prophetic proclamation of a hereafter, man's

profound and definite calling, in both continuity and
discontinuity with the present situation: beyond time
and history, beyond the transient reality of this
world, and beyond the things of this world, of
which a hidden dimension will one day be
revealed—beyond man himself, whose true destiny
is not restricted to his temporal aspect but will be
revealed in the future life. Evangelization therefore
also includes the preaching of hope in the promises
made by God in the new Covenant in Jesus Christ,
the preaching of God's love for us and of our love
for God; the preaching of brotherly love for all—
the capacity of giving and forgiving, of self-denial,
of helping one's brother and sister—which, spring-
ing from the love of God, is the kernel of the
Gospel; the preaching of the mystery of evil and the
active search for good. The preaching likewise—
and this is always urgent—of the search for God
himself through prayer which is principally that of
adoration and thanksgiving, but also through communion with the visible sign of the encounter with
God which is the Church of Jesus Christ; and this
communion in its turn is expressed by the application of those other signs of Christ living and acting
in the Church which are the sacraments. To live the
sacraments in this way, bringing their celebration to
a true fullness, is not, as some would claim, to
impede or to accept a distortion of evangelization:
it is rather to complete it. For in its totality,
evangelization—over and above the preaching of a
message—consists in the implantation of the
Church, which does not exist without the driving
force which is the sacramental life culminating in
the Eucharist. (EN 28)

Evangelizing through dialogue

Finally, by what means does Paul VI suggest we confront the modern world? The answer is clear. Mission today must always, and because of the nature of the Church, necessarily involve dialogue. In his first encyclical *Ecclesiam Suam*, Paul VI outlined a fourfold dialogue of the Church—with the world, with other faiths, with other Christians and internally, as he put it, 'between members of a community founded upon love' (ES 114). His insights were taken up and developed by the Second Vatican Council in such documents as 'The Church in the Modern World', 'Missionary Activity and Non-Christian Religions', 'Ecumenism', 'The Church and Eastern Catholic Churches'. In all these seminal documents dialogue is either explicitly referred to or is the presupposition implicit in them.

In theory at least dialogue could be one of many ways in which the Church relates to society and to others and conducts its own internal relationships. Pope Paul implicitly rejected two theoretical alternatives with regard to the world: the Church might, in his words,

> content itself with conducting an inquiry into the evils current in secular society, condemning them publicly and fighting a crusade against them. On the other hand, it might approach secular society with a view to exercising a preponderant influence over it and subjecting it to a theocratic power . . . (ES 78)

Obviously there is little point to the first and little practical possibility of the second. However, we who have inherited the traditions of a Christian Europe must beware of the temptation to long nostalgically for the restoration of Christendom, even locally, or to harbour the delusion that anything less is an evil to be combated.

On the contrary—and this is of immense importance—
Pope Paul asserts that dialogue is necessitated,

> by the prevalent understanding of the relationship
> between the sacred and the profane. It is demanded
> by the pluralism of society and by the maturity man
> has reached in this day and age. Be he religious or
> not, his secular education has enabled him to think
> and speak and conduct a dialogue with dignity.
> (ES 78)

There is no reason to believe that over the last thirty-
five years the human race has significantly regressed. The
pluralism of society is now even more pronounced, and
demands that dialogue suggested by *Gaudium et Spes* in
which the Church is urged to listen and receive as much
as it offers and speaks. Dialogue should not be mistaken
for monologue. So whatever may have been true in the
past, dialogue is today pre-eminently the style best suited
to modern times.

Yet far from being merely a convenient tactic, dialogue
for the Church has to be seen as 'modelled on the
dialogue of salvation'. In that dialogue there is revelation
and the individual's free response, in the presence of
which 'we dare not entertain any thoughts of external
coercion' (ES 75). The Council's affirmation of this understanding of divine revelation and religious freedom emphasizes the Trinitarian dialogue by which God unfolds
himself to his human creation, and also the free response
of men and women, whose enquiry into truth demands
'the aid of teaching . . . communication and dialogue' (ES
3). So dialogue corresponds to the pattern of the divine
economy, and it respects both God's revelation and the
dignity and freedom of the human person.

To lay such stress on dialogue might seem to undermine
the understanding we used to have of mission, which was
seen largely as a matter of proclamation and witness. It is
clear that dialogue in itself is not directly aimed at

'conversion to the true faith'—at least not as its first objective. Dialogue is nonetheless a way of evangelizing, a first step, to show the richness of God's revelation. It is possible to resolve the apparent tension at a deeper level.

We have to agree that the mission of the Church and of all the Church's members, is not in a sense their own mission at all; it is Christ's mission and is, therefore, God's mission. At a particular moment in time, Christ appointed the Apostles and their successors to carry on his mission on earth, but he did not then simply depart and leave the rest to them. He still conducts his mission now and his headship of the Church is effectively exercised through the outpouring on us of the Holy Spirit. Without that outpouring we would not be his Body and he could not carry out his mission. So it was not a once-for-all act of the past.

But dialogue is our human mode, in particular, by which we enable Christ to carry out his mission. We do not, as yet, possess the whole truth—all Christian history is a gradual exploration of it under the inspiration of the Spirit. The Church is constantly developing in its understanding of revelation (*Dei Verbum* 5). And so the dialogue is our proper mode of operation in order to enlarge our understanding and deepen our awareness as conscious instruments of Christ's mission.

The presence of the Kingdom and of uncovenanted—and sometimes surprising—grace in the world, means that we have to learn as well as teach, listen as well as speak. Respect for others, recognition of the 'seeds of the Gospel' planted throughout human society, consciousness that the whole of creation is made from the beginning in the Word, all lead us to a deeper and truer understanding of the Word and the Church and of its mission and the role of the laity in it. Only in this context and in these terms can we address ourselves to the renewal of the Church; only with this vision can we offer hope and the Good News of the Gospel to Europe today.

Christ's missionaries, the laity

In the depths of European consciousness today, it is possible to discern a profound change and the dawning of a realization that we are entering a new phase of history. The Age of Enlightenment has evidently run its course. This idea was explored by Lesslie Newbigin in a paper produced for the old British Council of Churches entitled 'Beyond 1984'. He maintained that we are currently experiencing the spiritual bankruptcy of Western society; beyond all doubt we have seen the limits of human reason as a means for exploring religious truth and for establishing an alternative value-system to the revealed truth of Christianity. At the same time we have been brought to the brink of destruction and have seen that technological mastery is no substitute for spiritual and moral maturity. We have now glimpsed what our future might become. So we do need to find a new and better way forward. This must involve every level of society. The political will has to be found to adopt solutions with vigour and determination. The Church plays its part in this process. It can never work alone or in isolation from all those other institutions and individuals whose contribution to the healing and rebuilding of society is so crucial. The Church has to take seriously and pursue with faith and determination that renewal whose essential elements were agreed at the Second Vatican Council. It must also, as Pope John Paul II so insistently reminds us, find new and effective ways of evangelizing today's world.

The need for apostles

Renewal and re-evangelization are, therefore, essential if the Church is to undertake effectively her mission in the world. These two are inextricably linked: there can be no effective evangelization without an authentic renewal—by which I mean that change of heart of which the gospel speaks so insistently—and renewal leads, inevitably, to sharing the gospel message with others. Structural changes of themselves do not effect conversion and renewal. To discover how spiritual renewal is brought about is the major need of our time. The fact that an increasing number are aware of this is, perhaps, a small beginning.

The process of renewal has already begun. Re-evangelization, on the other hand, is a task only now becoming evident. Although the needs of the modern world were deeply felt in the 1960s, it is only now becoming obvious how depleted is the spiritual and religious heritage of the Western world and how urgently needed is a radical evangelization of our society. We are, as Catholics, approaching this undertaking somewhat hesitantly. We have grown accustomed in Europe to devoting our pastoral efforts to maintenance rather than to mission. We can be excused for feeling daunted at the size and complexity of what is needed. We require accurate analysis of the contemporary situation. We need a more consistent and

energetic response if our generation is to hear the gospel
of Jesus Christ. The letter of Pope John Paul II to the
Presidents of the Bishops' Conferences of Europe
(2 January 1986), leaves us in no doubt as to the urgency
and importance of this task. He says:

> The profound and complex cultural, political, ethi-
> cal and spiritual transformations that have given a
> new face to the fabric of European society must be
> matched by a new quality of evangelization such as
> will succeed in setting before modern men and
> women the ageless message of salvation in convinc-
> ing terms. Europe needs to be given a soul and a
> new self-awareness. (6)

Faced with the reality of this ancient and complex
continent, we could be forgiven for feeling a sense of
despair as we contemplate the magnitude of our task. Yet
there is no mistaking the prospect which lies before us.
No longer is our continent united in the Christian faith,
rich in its spiritual heritage and so secure in its allegiance
to Christ that it can send out its sons and daughters to
preach Christ to a pagan world. Now much of Europe
has fallen from belief. Many of our own countries need
to have Christ preached and put before them as if they
were hearing of him for the first time. Europe needs
apostles. Europe needs Christians who will live their faith
and be witnesses to its truth. Europe needs men and
women to bring Christ into all walks of life, into their
homes and schools, into commerce and politics, into
social and intellectual life.

Throughout Christian history, the Church of Christ
has faced many crises. Each has brought forth from the
Church a response of faith which has been positively
enriching. In the first centuries of its existence the Church
was even then engaged in a painful process of clarifying
the content of its doctrines. It confronted within its own
ranks heresies and dissent and created a wealth of under-

standing which is still preserved for us in the creeds and in the writings of the Fathers. As Christian communities were submerged under waves of barbarism, monastic communities held on to precious learning and gradually evangelized and civilized their conquerors. When the Church became rich and complacent, St Dominic and St Francis recalled it to evangelical simplicity and austerity. After the Reformation new orders arose to implement the decrees of the Council of Trent and to spread its spirit. In the Age of Enlightenment, as literacy spread and schools were opened to educate children of every class, then the teaching orders sprang up to provide Christian education throughout Europe. And now, in our own time, at the end of the twentieth century, there is no doubt that to face the irreligion and unbelief of our time, to face sheer materialism and the cult of consumerism, the new apostles of our age must be Christian lay men and women.

In recent years we have come better to understand the nature of the Church as *koinonia* or *communio*. This approach has the advantage of rooting the life of the Church firmly in the mystery of God. The primary *koinonia*, from which the Church draws its life, is the Trinity itself. Each of the baptized is signed with the Trinity, not only to be incorporated individually into Christ, but also to be identified with the whole community of the redeemed who, being made one in Christ, are loved by the Father in the Spirit as the one Body of Christ. This has social or communal consequences as profound as those which are personal and individual.

Walter Kasper has pointed out that *communio* or *koinonia*,

> does not refer to the Church's structure, but to her essence, or, as the Council says, to her *mysterium*. The *aggiornamento* of the Council consisted precisely in this: in contrast to the one-sided concentration on the visible and hierarchical form of

the Church, it placed her mystery into the fore-
ground again, her mystery which can only be
grasped in faith. This is why the first part of the
Constitution on the Church is carefully entitled, *De
ecclesiae mysterio*.[1]

Now the Church as *koinonia* is called into being by the
Word of God received and acted upon in faith. All
believers, by virtue of baptism, become members of the
Body of Christ and share his mission. The primary identity of lay people comes from their baptismal calling into
the community of faith.

> From the fact of their union with Christ, the head,
> flows the lay-person's right and duty to be apostles.
> Inserted as they are into the Mystical Body of Christ
> by baptism and strengthened by the power of the
> Holy Spirit in confirmation, it is by the Lord himself
> that they are assigned to the apostolate. (AA 22)

Priesthood and prophecy

The Son of God became truly man, was flesh and blood,
entered our history and became part of our human story.
He redeemed humanity from within, from where he found
himself in time and place. The consequence is that the
Christian, like Christ, cannot regard the here and now as
irrelevant. The Christian, like Christ, is sent to this world
at this time with a mission and a ministry. The Christian
helps to redeem the world but must first be part of it. It is
the role of the Christian to suffer with others and for
others, just as it is the role of the Church to be in the
world and for the world. There is no place here for the
suggestion that the Church and the Christian can ignore
the contemporary scene and fix their eyes exclusively on
the next life.

The identification of the Christian with Christ extends beyond this basic fact of incarnation and presence. The Christian, through baptism, also shares in the work of Christ as priest, prophet and king. Here, I believe, can be found the special contribution of the Christian to the future of our continent—and, consequently, to the whole of society.

The whole Church at different levels is concerned with fulfilling its priestly mission. Each of the baptized, whether ordained or lay, share in different ways, as we all know, in the priesthood of Jesus Christ. St Peter, we recall, says to the People of God: 'You are a chosen race, a royal priesthood, a consecrated nation, a people set apart to sing the praises of God who called you out of darkness into his wonderful light' (1 Pet. 2.9). This priestly role involves the communal celebration of the Eucharist, the re-presenting to God of Christ's sacrifice which reconciles man and woman to God. That adoration, thanksgiving, and intercession offered by the whole People of God is, when properly understood, of the most profound importance to the human family. It creates and expresses community. It bridges the abyss between God and ourselves. It reconciles us to each other in a communal meal which is both a sacrifice and a healing.

The priesthood of the baptized goes further. It finds expression also in the signs and symbols of life. In this way, the Christian explores and intensifies the deeper experience of what it means to be human. Again, there is the daily personal relationship with God which exists through prayer and is nourished by it. Here once more all the baptized in their priestly role represent the whole of humankind when they pray; through Christ, with Christ and in Christ they offer prayer, praise and constant intercession for the needs of themselves and their neighbours.

Perhaps unfashionably, in an age of social concern and action, I would claim that the priestly role of the Christian and of the whole People of God is the most essential for the coherence of our society, for its well-being and for its spiritual and psychic health. Uprooted and superficial as we have become individually, we have lost, too, our sense of identity with each other in community. The priesthood of each Christian, consciously embraced, can serve to restore awareness of the transcendent and a sense of true community and can help society to rebuild its hierarchy of human values and priorities. But the awareness of the transcendent is the most important of all.

The baptized also share Christ's role as prophet. It means that Christians can never shed responsibility for proclaiming the Good News of Jesus Christ, in season and out of season, to those who hear and heed the Word and to those who reject it perhaps even with anger. It means as well that Christians have to interpret sensitively all human experience in the light of the gospel so that through them ordinary men and women can discover for themselves its deeper significance. And it means, finally, holding up to society the mirror of truth so that it can see its real features in the light of the Gospel. In that sense, it purifies and reveals at one and the same time.

If we believe that Jesus Christ is the truth and the light, then the teaching role of his followers involves bringing to the whole of society the truth that sets us free. The value, then, of the Christian's contribution to society by teaching, proclaiming and witnessing to the truth is again of immense importance. Community depends on communication, and communication of its nature has to be truthful. Community and society wither when falsehood flourishes. Truth is indivisible and, in the last analysis, truth is God. The Christian—as witness to truth, as defender of every genuine human value—can and should exercise a salutary influence in the field of education and in the public life of any nation.

The wealth of wisdom and experience contained in divine revelation and in the tradition of the Church is at the service of mankind. This *diaconia* of truth is so often brushed aside by society. Yet the modern world, and our continent as a whole, can draw light and inspiration from the current emphasis in Pope John Paul's teaching on the dignity of the human person. It is a theme which runs through the encyclicals of his pontificate. The Pope's preoccupation with the human person and human dignity is rooted in his experience in Poland when Communism and Christianity expressed fundamentally opposed views on the human person and yet found there common ground for discussion and discovery. Precisely here, in profound reflection on human existence, the Christian can make a special contribution to society. As Pope John Paul himself once said:

> Perhaps one of the most obvious weaknesses of present-day civilization lies in an inadequate view of man ... It is the drama of man being deprived of an essential dimension of his being, namely the search for the infinite, and thus faced with having his very being reduced in the worst way. (Puebla, 28 January 1979)

If the Christian today takes seriously his or her prophetic role, then he or she has already a rich store of doctrine and reflection on the current state of the world. There are, in particular, the documents of the Second Vatican Council and especially *Lumen Gentium* and *Gaudium et Spes*. Pope John Paul, at the beginning of his pontificate, said that these would be the twin pillars of his ministry. The Council can be studied in the light of subsequent synods which have sought to explore areas of urgent concern. In 1971 the Synod of Bishops reflected on the questions of justice and peace; in 1974, on evangelization; in 1977, on catechetics; and in 1980, on the family and its problems. The Christian can also reflect on the encyclicals of recent Popes and their teaching which interprets the present situation through the eyes of faith.

In pursuit of a prophetic role, the modern Christian would hardly dare to talk down to contemporary society. Lecturing is not a form of communication acceptable to people today. Instead, the Christian makes the most effective contribution by humbly initiating dialogue with others, dialogue within the Church, dialogue with other Christians.

The kingly role of the Christian

Finally, the Christian is called by God in baptism to share the kingship of Christ. That kingship knows nothing of triumphalism and domination. Christ the King carried a crown of thorns and was raised up on the throne of a cross. The Christian as king renounces coercion and demonstrates that the first shall be last and the last first. The Christian can provide contemporary Europe with a radical alternative to the pursuit of power; it involves trust in the presence and power of God and unswerving commitment to the gospel of love.

Christians, sharing the kingship of Christ, have to put other people first, have to affirm their dignity and maintain their rights. They have to wrestle with the agonizing problems of contemporary life which weigh so heavily on the conscience. They need to be in the forefront of the struggles for human rights and religious freedom. They need to face the dilemmas of defence and disarmament. How can society justify the vast sums devoted to the weapons of death? If we attach absolute value to the unborn innocent threatened by abortion, how can we contemplate without revulsion the possible destruction of countless millions and uncontrollable genetic damage to future generations? Chistians must make up their minds whether it is prudent or justifiable to urge their own country to disarm unilaterally if others do not or will not do so. They have further to decide whether the policy of deterrence, the conditional threat to use nuclear weapons, is morally defensible. The answers to these questions are not yet clear, since Christians defend opposing views.

I believe that the final Christian answer will consist in an uncompromising rejection of nuclear weapons and a campaign for total disarmament. Those Christians who conscientiously defend the nuclear deterrent (and this point of view must at this stage be respected), seem nonetheless to accept the present position reluctantly and conditionally as the lesser of possible evils. But the eventual outlawing of all nuclear weapons by all nations is the inescapable obligation of all of us towards humanity. Such a policy presupposes the goodwill of the international community and a binding commitment by the world's leaders to disarmament.

Again, Christians, sharing the kingship of Christ, cannot close their eyes to the enormous disparity between rich and poor nations in the world, between the Northern and the Southern hemispheres. They have to reject the injustice which underlies that disparity. They must choose, in countless practical and political ways, between personal profit and the welfare of the people. They must be prepared to accept a more frugal life if that is necessary to bring about a more just economic order. They know in their hearts that a Christian cannot serve both God and mammon.

The Christian has to accept the responsibility of stewardship, both for the finite resources of planet earth and for the humane use of those resources for the common good. The Christian, following Christ, makes a positive option for poverty and powerlessness. It is here that he is likely to come into conflict with the spirit of the age. The implications are endless; they are also urgent.

The Christian, too, must serve and reverence those despised by society. Nowhere has this to be done more urgently and sensitively than in the care of those handicapped physically and mentally. In Britain, there is a

tendency to sit in judgement on the quality of life possible
for others. Yet the Christian remembers that the physically handicapped share in a special way the suffering of
Christ, and believes that the mentally handicapped, sinless
in God's sight, are a creation of his love which we cannot
understand, but must unfailingly revere. We may well
discover that those regarded by us as the last as we
evaluate people, will turn out to be the first as God
estimates them. God's thoughts are not ours.

The struggle for the Kingdom is not an abstract conflict. It has to be fought here and now, in conditions
dictated by history and contemporary needs. And so we
have to contend with the problems of our age, while we
try, as best we can, to empty ourselves of the will to
dominate and rely instead on the invincible power of
divine love. We must be ready to dialogue and be flexible.
We must never lose patience or hope. We must be ready
to initiate and be positive, not simply to react defensively
and belatedly.

True human wisdom is to recognize that God alone is
absolute and the demands he makes upon us are unconditional. All else pales into relative insignificance before the
realization that he is our all, the beginning and end of all
creation, and that without him we can do nothing. No
good will ever be achieved until we acknowledge him and
confess before him our smallness and inadequacy. Once
we do that, then we are ready to receive more fully the
grace promised in our baptism, ready to become more
effectively priest, prophet, and king.

Notes

1. From Walter Kasper.

Come, Lord Jesus

*From the fig tree learn its lesson: as soon as its
branch becomes tender and puts forth its leaves,
you know the summer is near. So also, when you
see these things taking place, you know that he is
near, at the very gates.* (Mark 13.28)

Throughout history people have bewailed the sins of
their generation and the corruption of society and have
prophesied the imminent collapse of civilization. It requires little insight to detect the onset of winter; the tell-
tale signs of spring and new birth are, however, more
difficult to detect.

The witness and enduring values of St Benedict are a
beacon for those who see the work of European unity as
something more than the creation of a commercial free
market. There is at stake a deeper, more lasting, more
spiritual quest. Europe will never be wholly free nor
truly peaceful unless there is healing and wholeness
for wounded individuals and societies at odds with

themselves. The very essence of the Benedictine vision is the search for God by individuals within a community and by the community itself. Worship and praise of God is central, nourished by attentive reflection on the Word of God. Out of that springs authentic community and a way of life which is profoundly Christian. It should always be remembered that Benedict and his first communities were lay and their way of life a reflection of that spontaneous community we read about in the Acts of the Apostles. The first believers in Jerusalem were 'faithful to the teaching of the Apostles, to the brotherhood, to the breaking of bread and to the prayers' (Acts 2.42).

It is obvious that secular political and social groupings will never consciously model themselves on such ideals. But the memory of such communities emphasizes that without vision the people perish, and that society must nurture the whole person and attend to spiritual and psychic health as well as to material well being. The Benedictine experience shows it can be done.

It is surely highly significant that the prevailing unbelief and moral chaos of our time are being challenged by movements of the Spirit as dynamic as any in history. In all kinds of ways (of which the charismatic renewal is one), the Christian people today are rediscovering the reality of God's life and energy within them. There is a hunger for God, for prayer and the inner life which transcends denominational boundaries and is leading to a search for that holiness of life which is central to Christianity. The emptiness and despair so characteristic of our time must eventually yield, I believe, to the fulfilment and hope which is to be found in Jesus Christ.

It is also significant that today we are witnessing a rediscovery of the Church's social teaching, still too little known. This contains elements which throughout the past century have been—and are being—developed to provide a new and valid agenda for political and social reform.

Pope Paul VI set out that programme when he wrote: 'It is a question of building a world where everyone regardless of race, religion or nationality can live a fully human life, freed from servitude imposed by others or by natural forces over which he or she has insufficient control, a world where freedom is not an empty word and where the poor man Lazarus can sit down at table with the rich man' (PP 47).

The assertion that the gospel is both eternal and contemporary should come as no surprise. It is surely an incomplete and misguided religious faith which sees Christianity entirely in terms of the other-worldly or exclusively as philanthropic and politically involved. There has to be a finely-tuned balance and a comprehensive vision which results from a proper understanding of the Gospel.

It was a lawyer whose question elicited from Jesus Christ the precise statement on which Christian tradition has built up its understanding of our relationship to God and each other. Asked which of the 613 distinct commandments in the Law was the greatest, Jesus replied in effect that there is but a single imperative operating at two levels. The command to love embraces both God and neighbour. His linking of the two was unique and illuminating.

In fact any attempt to divorce the two or to emphasize one at the expense of the other leads to unreality and untruth. It distorts the Christian message. Both loves are but a single love. The notion that religion is a private and exclusively personal affair, concerned only with the eternal and other-worldly and with the after-life is, of course, too limited and thus erroneous. The idea that religion is mainly, or even exclusively, to do with attempting to effect social change or being heavily involved politically with little or no regard for the spiritual is also quite false.

Error is often the result of exaggerating a truth or of failing to maintain a proper balance between evident truths. It can also occur when we attempt to create a false dichotomy between things which are in reality one and the same.

From beginning to end the Bible consistently links the divine and the human, sees our daily behaviour as having consequences both physically and socially as well as spiritually and morally. At the heart of the Judaeo-Christian tradition are two basic convictions which shape all else. They are to be found in the first chapters of the Book of Genesis.

There is first and foremost the unwavering belief in the unique dignity of the human person. We are made—and this is a staggering assertion—in the very image and likeness of God. Each individual has a value that can never be lost and must never be ignored. This is the bedrock of our civilization. It explains our belief in the absolute sanctity of all human life and our constant concern for the rights and freedoms of each individual.

It is a principle which is today under constant and highly vocal attack. There is a widespread and intense campaign not only to legalize abortion but to present it as a fundamental right; age-old safeguards against the destruction of viable human life are being set aside in cases of handicap; human embryos are considered fit subject for destructive experimentation. The world has suffered this century from two of the worst dictatorships known to history. Torture and repression are still instruments of state control in many regimes. We tolerate appalling inequalities, widespread famine and crippling poverty in the southern hemisphere.

And there is secondly the conviction that all created things have a common origin, that all are the free gift of an ever-loving Father and all are intrinsically good. The human family is part of a greater whole, and destined consciously to be co-creative with the Father in the shaping of the world. We have the privilege and the responsibility not to dominate the rest of creation but to help it achieve its real purpose and goal.

Concern for the environment and for the prudent use of the planet's finite resources is still in its infancy. Human arrogance and indifference have caused havoc to our mother earth. We have failed conspicuously to realize our kinship with nature and other living things. Our future lies in a more humble and caring attitude to the creation of which we are truly part.

I believe that these fundamental convictions help us better to understand the link between loving and serving God and loving and relating to our neighbour. It is bound up, too, with a true appreciation of what it means to be authentically human.

All this is immediately relevant to the state of our world today and the ultimate destiny of the human family. Can anyone doubt that both at home and throughout our continent immense changes are under way? The ending of the Cold War and growing unity in Europe challenge us to create a new political and social order that will be just, peaceful, and compassionate. For that we need to develop ideals and values based on a true understanding of our very selves.

The future will not be secured by political tinkering or by social engineering and improved technology. What is needed is response to the centuries-old call of Christ to true conversion of heart and mind. There will be no better world without better people. And no better people without growth in genuine love. And there can be no growth in genuine love without faith in God and a true and lasting love of him.

Index